CAMBRIDGE
UNIVERSITY PRESS

Physics

for Cambridge IGCSE™

MATHS SKILLS WORKBOOK

Jane Thompson and Jaykishan Sharma

CAMBRIDGE
UNIVERSITY PRESS

University Printing House, Cambridge CB2 8BS, United Kingdom

One Liberty Plaza, 20th Floor, New York, NY 10006, USA

477 Williamstown Road, Port Melbourne, VIC 3207, Australia

314–321, 3rd Floor, Plot 3, Splendor Forum, Jasola District Centre, New Delhi – 110025, India

103 Penang Road, #05-06/07, Visioncrest Commercial, Singapore 238467

Cambridge University Press is part of the University of Cambridge.

It furthers the University's mission by disseminating knowledge in the pursuit of education, learning and research at the highest international levels of excellence.

www.cambridge.org
Information on this title: www.cambridge.org/9781108827355

Second edition 2018
Third edition 2022

20 19 18 17 16 15 14 13 12 11 10 9 8 7 6 5 4 3 2 1

Printed in Italy by L.E.G.O. S.p.A.

A catalogue record for this publication is available from the British Library

ISBN 978-1-108-82735-5 Maths Skills Workbook Paperback

Additional resources for this publication at www.cambridge.org/go

DEDICATED TEACHER AWARDS

Teachers play an important part in shaping futures. Our Dedicated Teacher Awards recognise the hard work that teachers put in every day.

Thank you to everyone who nominated this year; we have been inspired and moved by all of your stories. Well done to all of our nominees for your dedication to learning and for inspiring the next generation of thinkers, leaders and innovators.

Congratulations to our incredible winners!

WINNER

Regional Winner Middle East & North Africa	Regional Winner Europe	Regional Winner North & South America	Regional Winner Central & Southern Africa	Regional Winner Australia, New Zealand & South-East Asia	Regional Winner East & South Asia
Annamma Lucy GEMS Our Own English High School, Sharjah - Boys' Branch, UAE	**Anna Murray** British Council, France	**Melissa Crosby** Frankfort High School, USA	**Nonhlanhla Masina** African School for Excellence, South Africa	**Peggy Pesik** Sekolah Buin Batu, Indonesia	**Raminder Kaur Mac** Choithram School, India

For more information about our dedicated teachers and their stories, go to
dedicatedteacher.cambridge.org

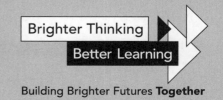

> Contents

> How to use this series

We offer a comprehensive, flexible array of resources for the Cambridge IGCSE™ Physics syllabus. We provide targeted support and practice for the specific challenges we've heard that learners face: learning science with English as a second language; learners who find the mathematical content within science difficult; and developing practical skills.

The coursebook provides coverage of the full Cambridge IGCSE Physics syllabus. Each chapter explains facts and concepts, and uses relevant real-world examples of scientific principles to bring the subject to life. Together with a focus on practical work and plenty of active learning opportunities, the coursebook prepares learners for all aspects of their scientific study. At the end of each chapter, examination-style questions offer practice opportunities for learners to apply their learning.

The digital teacher's resource contains detailed guidance for all topics of the syllabus, including common misconceptions identifying areas where learners might need extra support, as well as an engaging bank of lesson ideas for each syllabus topic. Differentiation is emphasised with advice for identification of different learner needs and suggestions of appropriate interventions to support and stretch learners. The teacher's resource also contains support for preparing and carrying out all the investigations in the practical workbook, including a set of sample results for when practicals aren't possible.

The teacher's resource also contains scaffolded worksheets and unit tests for each chapter. Answers for all components are accessible to teachers for free on the Cambridge GO platform.

The skills-focused workbook has been carefully constructed to help learners develop the skills that they need as they progress through their Cambridge IGCSE Physics course, providing further practice of all the topics in the coursebook. A three-tier, scaffolded approach to skills development enables learners to gradually progress through 'focus', 'practice' and 'challenge' exercises, ensuring that every learner is supported. The workbook enables independent learning and is ideal for use in class or as homework.

The practical workbook provides learners with additional opportunities for hands-on practical work, giving them full guidance and support that will help them to develop their investigative skills. These skills include planning investigations, selecting and handling apparatus, creating hypotheses, recording and displaying results, and analysing and evaluating data.

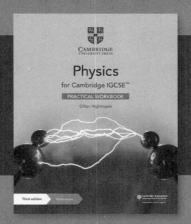

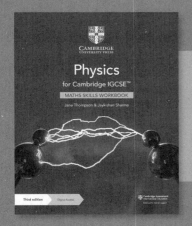

Mathematics is an integral part of scientific study, and one that learners often find a barrier to progression in science. The Maths Skills for Cambridge IGCSE Physics write-in workbook has been written in collaboration with the Association for Science Education, with each chapter focusing on several maths skills that learners need to succeed in their Physics course.

Our research shows that English language skills are the single biggest barrier to learners accessing international science. This write-in workbook contains exercises set within the context of Cambridge IGCSE Physics topics to consolidate understanding and embed practice in aspects of language central to the subject. Activities range from practising using comparative adjectives in the context of measuring density, to writing a set of instructions using the imperative for an experiment investigating frequency and pitch.

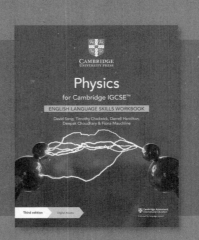

> How to use this book

Throughout this book, you will notice lots of different features that will help your learning. These are explained below.

OVERVIEW

- This sets the scene for each chapter, and explains why the maths skills in that chapter are important for you to understand.

WORKED EXAMPLE

These show a maths concept in action, giving you a step-by-step guide to answering a question related to that concept.

LOOK OUT

The information in these boxes will help you complete the questions, and give you support in areas that you might find difficult.

These boxes tell you where information in the book is extension content, and is not part of the syllabus.

Questions

Questions give you a chance to practise the skills in each Maths focus. You can find the answers to these questions in the Teacher's Resource.

EXAM-STYLE QUESTIONS

Questions at the end of each chapter provide more demanding exam-style questions. Answers to these questions can be found in the Teacher's Resource. Command words that appear in the syllabus and might be used in the exams are also highlighted in the exam-style questions. In the margin, you will find the Cambridge International definition.

APPLYING MORE THAN ONE SKILL

At the end of this Workbook you will find a section of exam-style questions covering any of the topics covered in the chapters. This will give you a chance to think about how to apply your maths skills to different contexts.

Throughout the book, you will see important words in **bold** font. You can find definitions for these words in the Glossary at the back of the book.

Supplement content

Where content is intended for students who are studying the Supplement content of the syllabus as well as the Core, this is indicated with the arrow and the bar, as you can see on the left here.

> Introduction

This workbook has been written to help you to improve your skills in the mathematical processes that you need in your Cambridge IGCSE™ Physics course. The exercises will guide you and give you practice in:

- representing values
- working with data
- drawing graphs
- interpreting data
- doing calculations
- working with shape.

Each chapter focuses on several maths skills that you need to master to be successful in your Physics course. It explains why you need these skills. Then, for each skill, it presents a step-by-step worked example of a question that involves the skill. This is followed by practice questions for you to try. These are not like exam questions. They are designed to develop your skills and understanding. They get increasingly challenging. Tips are often given alongside to guide you. Spaces, lines or graph grids are provided for your answers.

Understanding mathematics is critical to making sense of physics as physicists use equations to explain how one variable behaves in relation to others. For instance, knowing that speed = distance / time means that we can work out how the speed changes when the time is lengthened or shortened.

This book explains how data and graphs are interpreted by physicists. Once you have learned how to do it, you can apply the same method again and again in lots of different situations. Applying mathematics to physics is very methodical so it is worth learning how to do it.

Note for teachers:

Additional teaching ideas for this *Maths Skills Workbook* are available on Cambridge GO, downloadable with this workbook and the Cambridge IGCSE Physics Teacher's Resource. This includes engaging activities to use in lessons, with guidance on differentiation and assessment.

Answers to all questions in this *Maths Skills Workbook* are also accessible to teachers at www.cambridge.org/go

> Maths skills grid

The mathematical requirements focus on skills that you will need in your Cambridge IGCSE Physics course. Each of the mathematical requirements have been broken down for you with a reference to the chapters in this book that cover it. This will enable you to identify where you have practised each skill and also allow you to revise each one before your exams.

	Chapter 1	Chapter 2	Chapter 3	Chapter 4	Chapter 5	Chapter 6
Number						
add, subtract, multiply and divide						
use decimals, fractions, percentages, ratios and reciprocals	(decimals)	(decimals)	(decimals)			(decimals, fractions)
convert between decimals, fractions and percentages						
understand and use the symbols: =, <, >						
understand the meaning of sum, difference and product						
use standard form (scientific notation)						
understand that only the final answer in a calculation should be rounded						
use decimal places and significant figures appropriately						
make approximations and estimates to obtain reasonable answers						
Algebra						
use positive, whole number indices in algebraic expressions						
substitute values of quantities into equations, using consistent units						
solve simple algebraic equations for any one term when the other terms are known						
recognise and use direct and inverse proportion						
set up simple algebraic equations as mathematical models of physical situations and to represent information						

	Chapter 1	Chapter 2	Chapter 3	Chapter 4	Chapter 5	Chapter 6
Geometry and measurements						
understand the meaning of angle, curve, circle, radius, diameter, circumference, square, parallelogram, rectangle and diagonal			▓			▓
recall and use the equation for the circumference of a circle						▓
recall and use the equations for the area of a rectangle, area of a triangle and area of a circle						▓
recall and use the equations for the volume of a rectangular block and volume of a cylinder						▓
use scale diagrams						▓
apply Pythagoras' theorem to the calculation of a side of a right-angled triangle						
understand that a right angle is 90° and that the sum of the angles on a straight line is 180°						▓
use trigonometric functions (sine, cosine, tangent and their inverses)*					▓	
Graphs, charts and statistics						
draw graphs and charts from data			▓		▓	
interpret graphs and charts, including interpolation and extrapolation of data			▓		▓	
determine the gradient (slope) of a line on a graph, including* by drawing a tangent to a curved line			▓	▓		
determine the intercept of the line on a graph, extending the line graphically (extrapolating) where appropriate			▓	▓		
select suitable scales and axes for graphs			▓	▓		
understand that $y = mx + c$ represents a linear relationship				▓		
recognise direct proportionality from a graph					▓	
calculate and use the average (mean) for a set of data				▓		

Representing values

WHY DO YOU NEED TO REPRESENT VALUES IN PHYSICS?

- In physics, numbers are used to give values to measurable characteristics. We use the word **variable** for such a characteristic. Length, time and mass are just some of the variables whose values help us to describe features of the real world. For example, the time sunlight takes to reach the Earth is 8 minutes and 20 seconds, the mass of the of the moon is 7.3×10^{22} kg, the speed of a bullet train is 500 km/h, the mass of 1 litre of water is 1 kg.

- Each variable has a **unit** linked to it. The unit allows us to understand the size of the variable. Examples of units are: metres, seconds, kilograms and amps.

Maths focus 1: Using units

KEY WORDS

variable: the word used for any measurable quantity; its value can vary or change

unit: a standard used in measuring a variable, for example the metre or the volt

A measured value in physics means nothing without a unit. Scientists have agreed a set of standard units. Wherever you are in the world, scientists use the same set of standard units called SI units (*Système Internationale*). Imagine if you have only numbers in your life, without units. What would your life be like? Does it make sense if you ask a shopkeeper to give you 10 salts?

What maths skills do you need to be able to use units?

1	Choosing the correct unit for a variable	• Identify the variable
		• Recall the correct unit to match the variable
		• Use the correct symbol for the unit
		• Convert units

Maths skills practice

How does using the correct units help when working with equations?

Using the same units means that we can compare the size of variables and calculations very easily. This is why the international SI system was agreed. Table 1.1 shows the basic SI units for some variables. Each unit has a symbol, which makes the unit easier to recognise and write quickly.

Variable	SI unit	SI unit symbol
length (or distance)	metre	m
mass	kilogram	kg
time	second	s

Table 1.1: Units for length, time and mass.

Sometimes you will see different units used (see Table 1.2).

Variable	Unit
length (or distance)	kilometre, millimetre
time	hour

Table 1.2: Different units can be used for the same variable.

The unit metres per second (m/s) for speed is a 'derived unit', which means it is based on a calculation. It is the number of metres travelled in each second. The / symbol is read as 'per' and indicates division.

You can read more about SI units in Chapter 1 of the Coursebook.

Other SI units that you need to be familiar with are shown in Table 1.3.

Variable	SI unit
force	newton (N)
energy	joule (J)
power	watt (W)
temperature	degrees Celsius (°C)
frequency	hertz (Hz)
potential difference	volt (V)
electric current	ampere (A)
resistance	ohm (Ω)
electric charge	coulomb (C)

Table 1.3: SI units.

LOOK OUT

Be careful with units when using equations. For example, when distance and time are measured in metres and seconds, the speed that you calculate will be a value in m/s (metres per second), not in km/h (kilometres per hour).

Maths skill 1: Choosing the correct unit for a variable

In a calculation, the units you use must match (be consistent) with one another. For example, when calculating an area using the equation

area = length × width

the length and width must have the same units. When the length measurement is in centimetres (cm) and the width is in millimetres (mm), one must be converted so they are consistent.

In Figure 1.1, the width measurement has been converted from millimetres to centimetres.

Figure 1.1: Converting millimetres to centimetres.

The area is then 20 cm × 1 cm = 20 cm².

See Chapter 6, Maths focus 1, '*Solving problems involving shape*' for more on calculating area.

To convert from cm to m, from cm² to m², or from cm³ to m³, remember:

*   there are 100 cm in 1 m

*   there are 10 000 cm² in 1 m²

*   there are 1 000 000 cm³ in 1 m³.

The conversion factors are shown in Table 1.4.

Original unit	New unit	Process	Example
cm	m	Divide by 100	500 cm = 5 m
cm²	m²	Divide by 10 000	5000 cm² = 0.5 m²
cm³	m³	Divide by 1 000 000	50 000 cm³ = 0.05 m³

Table 1.4: Converting units of length, area and volume.

WORKED EXAMPLE 1.1

Find the volume of the block of material in Figure 1.2.

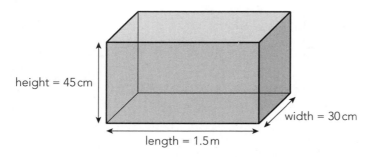

Figure 1.2: Block of material.

CONTINUED

Step 1: Remind yourself of the equation for volume.

Volume = length × width × height

Step 2: List each variable with its units.

Length = 1.5 m
Width = 30 cm
Height = 45 cm
Volume = ?

Step 3: Check for consistency and decide which unit you are going work in.
Here we will work in metres (remember that 1 cm = 0.01 m).

Length = 1.5 m
Width = 0.3 m
Height = 0.45 m
Volume = ?

Step 4: Substitute the values and units into the equation and find the volume.

Volume = 1.5 m × 0.3 m × 0.45 m
Volume = 0.20 m³

Questions

1 a A student releases a trolley down a long ramp, as shown in Figure 1.3. As the front of the trolley passes marker 1, she starts a stopwatch and stops it as the trolley reaches marker 2.

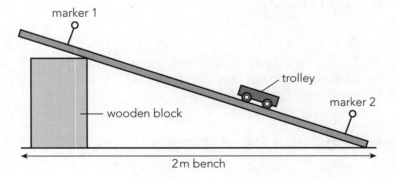

Figure 1.3: Trolley rolling down a ramp.

Write down suitable units, in symbols, for the following variables:

i The time taken to travel down the ramp is measured in ....

ii The length of the ramp is measured in ....

iii The mass of the trolley is measured in ....

b The distance between marker 1 and marker 2 is 1.6 m and it takes 2 s to cover this distance. Calculate the speed of the trolley. Give your answer in m/s.

....

....

....

2

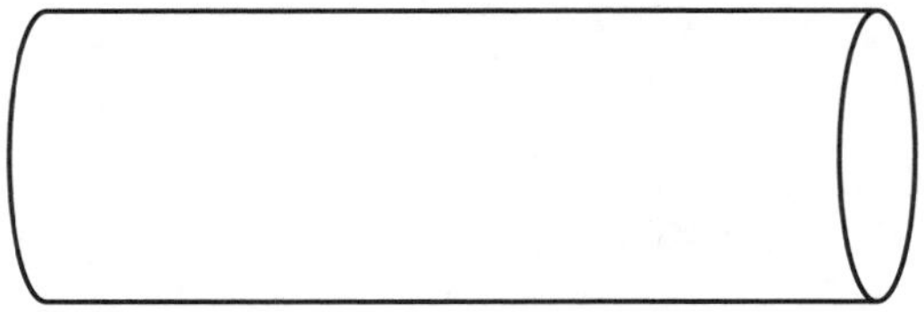

Figure 1.4: Horizontal cylinder.

A horizontal cylinder has a cross-sectional area of 30 cm² and a length of 3 m. What is its volume?

Use the equation volume = cross-sectional area × length

....

....

....

Do you need to convert the units? Why? Discuss with your classmate.

Maths focus 2: Using symbols for variables

A *variable* is a measurable characteristic. It has a value, expressed as a number with a unit. Scientists use symbols instead of the variable names and units to help find and work with relationships between variables. Then they can express the relationship as a mathematical equation.

What maths skills do you need to use symbols for variables?

1	Using the symbol for each variable and its unit	• Learn the symbol for each variable
		• Know that the symbol stands for the variable and its unit

Maths skills practice

How does using symbols for variables help you to learn and use equations in physics?

Look at this equation that shows the relationship between the mass of an object, the gravitational field strength and its weight:

weight (in N) = mass (in kg) × gravitational field strength (in N/kg)

Writing equations like this is slow and inefficient. Using symbols, this becomes faster and much easier:

$W = mg$

W stands for 'weight in N'. For example the value of W might be 10 N. The symbol includes the numerical value *and* the unit.

In symbol equations, the multiplication sign is often omitted: $mg = m \times g$

Maths skill 1: Using the symbol for each variable and its unit

Most variables in physics have symbols, which are single letters. You need to learn them. A few variables, such as a moment, have no symbol.

Practise your knowledge of symbols. Make yourself a set of flash cards with the variable name and symbol on one side, and the unit name and symbol on the other (Figure 1.5). Practise until you know them all.

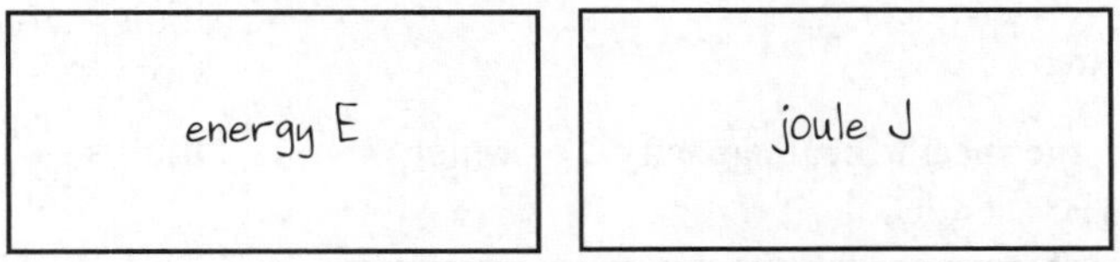

```
┌─────────────────────┐   ┌─────────────────────┐
│                     │   │                     │
│                     │   │                     │
│      energy E       │   │      joule J        │
│                     │   │                     │
│                     │   │                     │
└─────────────────────┘   └─────────────────────┘
```

Figure 1.5: Each side of one flashcard, used to help you remember variable symbols and units.

There are only 26 letters in the alphabet, so sometimes the same letter is used more than once.

- Sometimes lower case (small) letters are used and sometimes upper case (CAPITALS):
    - m represents both metre and milli (the prefix for 10^{-3}); m represents mass.
    - V represents volt; V represents both volume and potential difference.

- In print, *italic* single letters are always variables; units are shown in ordinary type. For example, A means area but A means amp.

- Sometimes Greek letters are used. For example, θ for temperature in °C.

WORKED EXAMPLE 1.2

Read this paragraph about heating water and fill the gaps by writing the correct symbols after each **bold** term.

A 1 **kilogram** .... mass of water is heated from a temperature of

5 **degrees Celsius** .... to 100 **degrees Celsius** ....

The heater has a **power** .... of 50 **watts** .... i.e. it delivers

50 **joules per second** ....

The heater has to be connected to a 24-**volt** .... supply.

An amount of **energy** .... is used to heat the water.

The temperature rise of the water depends on the **specific heat capacity** ....

of water, measured in **joules per kilogram degree Celsius** ....

Step 1: Make sure you know the proper symbols. Never make up symbols.

Step 2: Take care to use lower and upper case letters correctly.

Step 3: Make sure you know when you need a / symbol.

Check your answers below.

A 1 **kilogram** kg mass of water is heated from a temperature of 5 **degrees Celsius** $°C$ to 100 **degrees Celsius** $°C$.

The heater has a **power** P of 50 **watts** W i.e. it delivers 50 **joules per second** J/s.

The heater has to be connected to a 24-**volt** V supply.

An amount of **energy** E is used to heat the water.

The temperature rise of the water depends on the **specific heat capacity** c of water, measured in **joules per kilogram degree Celsius** $J/(kg\,°C)$.

LOOK OUT

The brackets in J/(kg °C) show that joules are divided by both kg and °C, that is $\dfrac{J}{kg\,°C}$.

Questions

3   The electric power needed for a kettle can be found by using the equation:

power = potential difference × current

Complete the table to show the correct symbols for the variables and names and symbols for the units.

Variable	Symbol for the variable	Name of unit	Symbol for unit
power			
potential difference			
current			

4

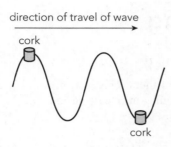

Figure 1.6: Corks on a water wave.

A student places two corks in a bowl of water. The student uses a ruler and a stopwatch to take measurements as a water wave moves across the surface (Figure 1.6). Which line in Table 1.5 gives the correct variable symbols and units for the measurements and average speed calculations?

Circle A, B, C or D.

	Speed		Distance		Time	
	Variable symbol	Unit symbol	Variable symbol	Unit symbol	Variable symbol	Unit symbol
A	*v*	cm/s	*d*	cm	*t*	s
B	*s*	m/s	*D*	m	*t*	s
C	*s*	cm/s	*d*	m	*T*	s
D	*v*	m/s	*s*	m	*T*	s

Table 1.5: Measurements on a water wave for Question 4.

5   A digital radio is 90% efficient. The radio is powered by chemical energy from the Sun transferred as light through solar cells.

a   Write the correct variable symbol, unit symbols and unit names in the table.

Variable	Symbol for the variable	Name of unit	Symbol for unit
power			
energy			

b   An equation for efficiency is:

$$\text{efficiency} = \frac{\text{useful energy out}}{\text{energy input}} \times 100\%$$

Explain why efficiency has a % sign rather than units.

....

....

....

Maths focus 3: Determining significant figures

Some figures (digits) in a number are more important than others. This section is about how to decide which parts of a number are most significant in calculations and when estimating.

What maths skills do you need to determine significant figures?

1	Understanding place value	• Compare the size of different numbers
		• Relate place value to the size of common measurements
2	Determining a correct number of significant figures	• Identify and count significant figures
		• State numbers to a required number of significant figures

Maths skills practice

How are significant figures useful in physics measurements?

The number of **significant figures** in a value indicates how precisely you know the number. For example, a measurement given as 2.34 m has three significant figures and means the measurement is known to the nearest 0.01 m (1 cm).

> **KEY WORDS**
>
> **significant figures:** the number of digits in a measurement, not including any zeros at the beginning; for example, the number of significant figures in 0.0682
> is three

See Chapter 2 for more on precision and accuracy.

Maths skill 1: Understanding place value

When we write numbers, the position (place) of each digit is important (see Figure 1.7).

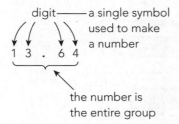

Figure 1.7: Digits in a decimal number.

The positions of the digits give you information about the value represented by the digits. Each place represents ten times the place to the right (Figure 1.8).

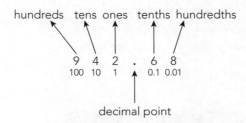

Figure 1.8: How place values are shown in decimal numbers.

Place values in measurements are very important because they indicate value in hundreds, tens and ones of each digit in a measurement. You can see in Figure 1.8 that the 4 in the number really means *4 tens*, or *40*, because of its position.

KEY WORDS

decimal place: the place-value position of a number after a decimal point; the number 6.357 has three decimal places

---

The number of digits after the decimal point indicates the number of **decimal places** in the number. In Figure 1.8, the number is given to two decimal places (2 d.p.).

WORKED EXAMPLE 1.3

A student must decide which resistor to use in his circuit. He has a box containing resistors with their resistance values marked (Figure 1.9).

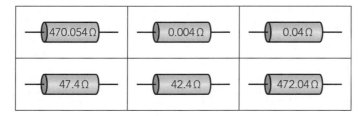

Figure 1.9: Box of fuses given to a student.

The student needs a resistor that is close to four hundredths of an ohm. Which one should he choose? Be clear of the difference between *thousands* (1000) and *thousandths* $\left(\frac{1}{1000}\right)$.

Step 1: Check that all of the resistances are expressed in the same unit, Ω or $k\Omega$. In this case, they are all in Ω. Comparisons are easier to make if the same units are used.

Step 2: Prepare a grid to hold the numbers.

100s	10s	1s	Decimal point	$\frac{1}{10}$	$\frac{1}{100}$	$\frac{1}{1000}$
			.			

Step 3: Always keeping the decimal points directly below one another, fill in the grid with all the values.

100s	10s	1s	Decimal point	$\frac{1}{10}$	$\frac{1}{100}$	$\frac{1}{1000}$
4	7	0	.	0	5	4
		0	.	0	0	4
		0	.	0	4	
	4	7	.	4		
	4	2	.	4		
4	7	2	.	0	4	

Step 4: Now that you can compare values, choose the one that is equal or closest to the value four hundredths of an ohm.

This is $0.04\,\Omega$.

You can read more about resistors in Chapter 19 of the Coursebook.

Questions

6 A student is writing down the power of appliances used in her home. Her results are shown in Figure 1.10.

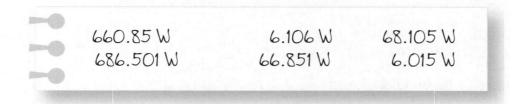

660.85 W   6.106 W   68.105 W
686.501 W   66.851 W   6.015 W

Figure 1.10: Horizontal cylinder.

a Which line shows increasing power from smallest to largest? Circle A, B, C or D.

It may help to draw a place value grid like that in Worked example 1.3.

A 686.501 W 660.85 W   68.105 W 66.851 W 6.106 W   6.015 W

B 6.015 W   6.106 W   66.851 W 68.105 W 660.85 W 686.501 W

C 68.105 W   6.106 W   660.85 W 66.851 W 686.501 W 6.015 W

D 6.106 W   6.015 W   68.105 W 66.851 W 660.85 W 686.501 W

100s	10s	1s	Decimal point	$\frac{1}{10}$	$\frac{1}{100}$	$\frac{1}{1000}$
			.			
			.			
			.			
			.			
			.			
			.			

b State which of the power figures could belong to a microwave cooker.

....

c State which of the power figures could belong to a mobile phone charger.

....

7 The melting point of mercury is stated to be −38.8290 °C. What fraction of a degree Celsius is this value precise to?

....

> **LOOK OUT**
>
> When reading negative numbers, as in a temperature of −7 °C, it is better to use the phrase 'a temperature of *negative* 7 °C'. Avoid using the word 'minus'; just use 'minus' for subtractions.

Maths skill 2: Determining a correct number of significant figures

When reading a number from left to right, the first *significant figure* is the first digit *other than zero*.

$$\downarrow$$
$$0.065\,00$$

The first significant figure is 6, which has the value $\dfrac{6}{100}$.

$$\downarrow$$
$$700\,560$$

The first significant figure is 7, which has the value 700 000.

Counting significant figures in numbers less than 1

To find the total number of significant figures, count the digits from left to right starting from the first significant figure.

$$\downarrow\downarrow\;\downarrow\downarrow$$
$$0.089\,04$$

The number 0.089 04 has four significant figures (4 s.f.).

Counting significant figures in large numbers

The zeros are written to give place value but are ignored when counting significant figures, unless they come between two other non-zero digits. The counting is again from left to right.

$$\downarrow\quad\downarrow\downarrow$$
$$900\,560\,000$$

The number 900 560 000 has five significant figures (5 s.f.)

Changing to a specified number of significant figures

Changing a number to a specified number of significant figures involves **rounding** (see Figure 1.11). For example, 546 520 written to two significant figures is 550 000.

> **KEY WORD**
>
> **rounding:** expressing a number as an approximation, with fewer significant figures; for example, 7.436 rounded to two significant figures is 7.4, or rounded to three significant figures it is 7.44

To decide the value of the *final significant figure* you either round the next digit up or down.

Consider the value of the next digit. Is it greater or less than 5?

If greater than or equal to 5:	If less than 5:
Increase the final significant figure by 1.	Keep the final significant figure the same.
Example	**Example**
546 520 rounded to two significant figures is 550 000.	542 480 rounded to two significant figures is 540 000.
The third figure, 6, has been rounded up to 10.	The third figure, 2, has been rounded down to 0.

Figure 1.11: Key steps when rounding.

WORKED EXAMPLE 1.4

In a density experiment, the volume of 12 marbles is found to be 6.2832 cm³. What is the volume of one marble to two significant figures?

Step 1: Divide 6.2832 cm³ by 12 = 0.5236 cm³

Step 2: In the number 0.5236, count from the left. Keep the zero before the decimal point; this is not counted as a significant figure.

$$\overset{\text{1st 2nd}}{\underset{\downarrow\ \downarrow}{}}$$
$$0.5\,2\,3\,6$$

Consider the value of the third significant figure. As 3 is below 5, it and all following numbers can be ignored.

Volume of one marble = 0.52 cm³ to 2 s.f.

Questions

8 Which of these energy values has been given to three significant figures?
   Circle A, B, C or D.

   A 4065 J   **B** 0.40 J   **C** 4060 J   **D** 0.41 J

9 Light travels at a constant speed of 2.99 792 × 10⁸ m/s in a vacuum.

   Round this value to:

   a two significant figures ....

   b four significant figures ....

10 Which is the correct result for rounding 14.58 to three significant figures?
   Circle A, B, C or D.

   A 1.458   **B** 14.580   **C** 14.5   **D** 14.6

Maths focus 4: Representing very large and very small values

Working with very large and very small numbers can be difficult. It is easy to make errors. Using **standard form (scientific notation)** helps reduce the number of mistakes and also makes it easier to write and compare measurements. For example, the mass of the Earth is:

5 972 000 000 000 000 000 000 000 kg

This number is more simply expressed as 5.972×10^{24} kg and also much easier to compare with, say, the mass of the sun: 1.989×10^{30} kg.

The mass of a single hydrogen atom is:

0.000 000 000 000 000 000 000 000 001 672 7 kg

This is much more easily expressed as 1.6727×10^{-27} kg.

Unit prefixes are another way of making it easier to show large and small values:

- The thickness of a piece of wire is easier to understand in millimetres, mm, than in metres.
- The length of an electricity cable between a power station and a town might be given in kilometres, km, rather than metres.

What maths skills do you need to represent very large and very small values?

1	Converting numbers to and from standard form	• Choose when to use standard form
		• Write large numbers in terms of a positive power of 10
		• Write small numbers in terms of a negative power of 10

2	Interpreting and converting values with unit prefixes to and from standard form	• Convert between unit prefix form and standard form
3	Carrying out arithmetic operations in standard form	• Know how to add, subtract, multiply and divide in standard form

Maths skills practice

How does using standard form help in describing the properties of electromagnetic waves?

The typical wavelength of ultraviolet light is 3.8×10^{-7} m. The typical wavelength of gamma rays is 5.7×10^{-11} m. When you are confident in interpreting standard form using negative powers of 10, it is easy to see that the wavelength of ultraviolet is longer than that of gamma rays. If these wavelengths were written as ordinary decimal numbers, it would be hard to count all those zeros.

The speed of all electromagnetic waves in a vacuum is 3.0×10^8 m/s. Using standard form for the speed v and the wavelength λ helps in applying the equation:

wave velocity = frequency × wavelength

$$v = f \times \lambda$$

It would be very easy to make an error if you write zeros.

Maths skill 1: Converting numbers to and from standard form

Standard form is used to express very large and very small numbers in a simpler format. This can help to highlight the significant figures:

543 520 in standard form becomes $5.435\,20 \times 10^5$

or 5.4×10^5 to two significant figures.

In standard form, *the decimal point is always placed after the first significant figure*.

Large numbers in standard form

KEY WORDS

power of ten: a number such as 10^3 or 10^{-3}

A number larger than 10 is written with a positive **power of ten** in standard form. How does 500 become 5×10^2 in standard form?

$500 = 5 \times 100$

$100 = 10 \times 10 \leftarrow$ multiply by 10 twice

$100 = 10^2$

so $500 = 5 \times 10^2$

500 and 5×10^2 are the same value, shown in different ways.

Numbers less than 1 in standard form

A number smaller than 1 is written with a negative power of 10 in standard form. How does 0.006 become 6×10^{-3} in standard form?

$$0.006 = 6 \times 0.001$$

$$0.001 = \frac{1}{10 \times 10 \times 10}$$

$$= 10^{-3} \leftarrow \text{divide by 10 three times}$$

so $0.006 = 6 \times 10^{-3}$

0.006 and 6×10^{-3} are the same value, shown in different ways.

KEY WORDS

index: a small number that indicates the power; for example, the index 4 here shows that the 2 is raised to the power 4, which means four 2s multiplied together: $2^4 = 2 \times 2 \times 2 \times 2$

power: a number raised to the power 2 is squared (e.g. x^2); a number raised to the power 3 is cubed (e.g. x^3); and so on

---

The **index** or **power** of 10 tells you how many times to use 10 in a multiplication or division (see Table 1.6).

10^2 is **10 × 10** = 100	10^{-2} is $\dfrac{1}{\mathbf{10 \times 10}} = \dfrac{1}{100}$ Expressed in decimal form as 0.01
10^5 is **10 × 10 × 10 × 10 × 10** = 100 000	10^{-5} is $\dfrac{1}{\mathbf{10 \times 10 \times 10 \times 10 \times 10}} = \dfrac{1}{100\,000}$ Expressed in decimal form as 0.000 01

Table 1.6: Different powers of ten

WORKED EXAMPLE 1.5

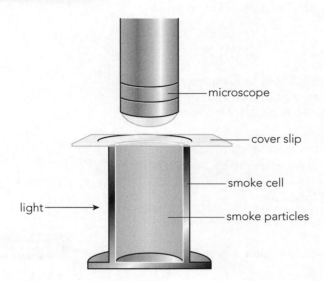

Figure 1.12: Observing Brownian motion.

In an experimental arrangement for observing Brownian motion (Figure 1.12), the particles of smoke are just large enough to be visible under the microscope.

KEY WORD

diameter: a straight line connecting two points on a circle (or sphere) that passes through the centre

The **diameter** of a smoke particle is 0.000 000 035 m. Express this in standard form.

Key question to ask yourself:

Does the process involve dividing or multiplying by 10 to get the power?

This depends on whether you are working with very large or very small numbers. In this case, the number is very small and therefore division by 10 is involved.

Step 1: Look at the groups of three digits in the number 0.000 000 035.
Reading from left to right, find the first digit that is non-zero.

$$\downarrow$$
$$0.000\,000\,035$$

The decimal point goes after this digit:

$$3.5$$

> **CONTINUED**

Step 2: Work out the decimal number you need to multiply 3.5 by to equal 0.000 000 035.

$$0.000\,000\,035 = 3.5 \times 0.000\,000\,01$$

Step 3: Find the power of 10 to be used when 0.000 000 01 is expressed in standard form, by finding how many times 1 has to be divided by 10 to become 0.000 000 01. Imagine moving the 1 to the right, place by place:

1.000 000 000

0.000 000 01

This shows that 1.0 has been divided by 10 eight times to become 0.000 000 01

It has to be divided by 10 a total of 8 times, so:

$$0.000\,000\,01 = 10^{-8}$$

Step 4: Substitute the power of 10 value into the equation in Step 3, to give the answer in standard form:

$$0.000\,000\,035\,\text{m} = 3.5 \times 10^{-8}\,\text{m}$$

> **LOOK OUT**
>
> Don't forget the unit in your final answer.

You can read more about Brownian motion in Chapter 9 of the Coursebook.

Questions

11 a What is standard form? Circle A, B, C or D.

    A Writing numbers as decimals

    B Writing numbers with zeroes

    C Writing numbers in fractions

    D A system of writing very large and very small values in simpler format

b Convert these numbers to standard form.

    i 56 752

    ....

    ii 253.312

    ....

    iii 1000.5

    ....

    iv 0.06

    ....

    v 0.000 446

    ....

12 Convert these values from standard form to numbers with zeros.

    a   Length of a year: 3.156×10^7 seconds.

    ....

    b   The ratio of proton to electron mass: 1.8362×10^3.

    ....

    c   The wavelength of red light: 6.5×10^{-7} m.

    ....

    d   The distance from the Earth to the Sun: 1.496×10^9 m
         Give your answer in kilometres.

    ....

Maths skill 2: Interpreting and converting values with unit prefixes to and from standard form

In physics, unit prefixes are often used to make measurement values easier to understand. A prefix is an addition to the beginning of a word to change its meaning. In the case of units, the prefix represents a multiple of 10. Look at the examples in Table 1.7. The prefix goes in front of the unit's name. The symbol for the prefix goes in front of the unit symbol.

Multiplying factor	Prefix	Standard form	Example
1 000 000 000	giga G	1×10^9	gigawatt GW
1 000 000	mega M	1×10^6	megajoule MJ
1000	kilo k	1×10^3	kilogram kg
1	*No prefix*	1×10^0	amp A
0.1	deci d	1×10^{-1}	decimetre dm
0.01	centi c	1×10^{-2}	centimetre cm
0.001	milli m	1×10^{-3}	millilitre ml
0.000 001	micro μ	1×10^{-6}	microcoulomb μC
0.000 000 001	nano n	1×10^{-9}	nanosecond ns

Table 1.7: The meanings of unit prefixes used in physics.

> ### WORKED EXAMPLE 1.6

Sometimes you will need to express small units in standard form, for example 0.01mm.

a Convert this value to metres, m.

b Give this value in standard form.

Step 1: Find the prefix m in Table 1.4, and look up the power of 10 in the standard form column: 1×10^{-3}.

Step 2: Remove the m in 0.01 mm and write a multiplication sign followed by 10 to the given power.

a 0.01 mm becomes 0.01×10^{-3} m.

b This is 1.0×10^{-5} m in standard form.

> **LOOK OUT**
>
> In standard form the decimal point always goes after the first significant figure.

Questions

13 The sun releases 3.85×10^{20} MJ energy per second. How many watts (W) is this, in standard form?

....

14 How many nanometres are there in 1 μm?

....

15 Convert the following values into the units given. Give your answers in standard form.

a 0.7 kW = ... W

b 14 ms = ... s

c 23 MΩ = ... Ω

d 1.8 μC = ... C

e 475 nm = ... m

Maths skill 3: Carrying out arithmetic operations in standard form

Adding and subtracting numbers in standard form

Take care when adding and subtracting numbers expressed in standard form. Unless you use a calculator with care, you can only easily add or subtract numbers with the same power of 10. Often the best method is to change the expression into ordinary numbers and add or subtract as normal.

Multiplying and dividing numbers in standard form

- The significant figures in a number follow normal rules for multiplication and division.

- Powers follow these rules:

  Multiplication of powers of 10: $10^a \times 10^b = 10^{a+b}$

  Division of powers of 10: $\dfrac{10^a}{10^b} = 10^{a-b}$

  Raising a power to a power: $(10^a)^b = 10^{ab}$

- A negative power indicates that the power is in the denominator: $10^{-a} = \dfrac{1}{10^a}$.

- Identity rule: Any non-zero number raised to the power of zero is equal to 1, for example: $10^0 = 1$.

Using standard form on a calculator

Take care when you put standard form into your calculator. What you press is not what you see! The EXP button on your calculator means '×10 to the power of'.

What would you press to enter 3.27×10^4 in your calculator?

You would press 3.27 then EXP (the exponent key) then 4.

Try it and see!

WORKED EXAMPLE 1.7

In the Solar System, Venus is 1.08×10^8 km away from the Sun. How long does sunlight take to reach the surface of Venus? The speed of light in a vacuum is 3.0×10^8 m/s. Give your answer in standard form.

Use the equation $\text{time} = \dfrac{\text{distance}}{\text{speed}}$

Step 1: Substitute the values into the equation.

$$\text{Time} = \frac{1.08 \times 10^{11}\,\text{m}}{3.0 \times 10^8\,\text{m/s}}$$

Key questions to ask yourself:

- Does this question involve addition or subtraction?

  No

- Does this question involve multiplication or division of powers of 10?

  Yes, division rules apply here.

Step 2: First divide 1.08 by 3.0.

$$\frac{1.08}{3.0} = 0.36$$

So you have

$$\text{time} = \frac{0.36 \times 10^{11}}{10^8}$$

CONTINUED

Step 3: Use the division of powers rule: $\dfrac{10^a}{10^b} = 10^{a-b}$

Time $= 0.36 \times 10^{11-8}$

density $= 0.36 \times 10^3\,\text{s}$

Step 4: Change to standard form (one figure before the decimal point).

Time $= 3.6 \times 10^2\,\text{s}$

See Maths focus 3, Maths skill 2 for more on significant figures and rounding.

Questions

16 a Express 1 millimetre (mm) in metres (m) in standard form.

1 mm = ...

b Proxima Centauri b, an exoplanet orbiting in the habitable zone of the red dwarf star Proxima Centauri, which is the closest star to the Sun and part of a triple star system, is located approximately 4.2 light-years from Earth. (1 light-year $= 9.5 \times 10^{15}\,\text{m}$)

Express the distance in kilometres, in standard form.

....

....

....

17 An air conditioner draws 6900 mA current when connected to a $2.4 \times 10^2\,\text{V}$ mains supply. Calculate the power consumed by the air conditioner. Use the equation: $P = V \times I$

....

....

18 A TV station transmits a signal at a frequency of 500 MHz. The speed of transmitted waves in air is $3.0 \times 10^8\,\text{m/s}$. Find the wavelength of the signal.

Use the equation:

wave speed = frequency × wavelength

rearranged as:

$$\text{wavelength} = \frac{\text{wave speed}}{\text{wave frequency}}$$

Give your answer in standard form.

....

....

....

LOOK OUT

Do not forget to replace the unit prefix with the correct multiple of 10 before you substitute the values into the equation.

Maths focus 5: Estimating values

KEY WORDS

estimate: (find) an approximate value

order of magnitude: the approximate size of a number, often given as a power of 10; for example, the order of magnitude of 2700 is 10^3

An important aspect of physics is being able to tell if the numbers shown on a calculator are giving you roughly the right answer. **Estimating** is a technique for checking.

Imagine you get an answer for a car's speed as 70 km/s. Should a car travel at 70 km/s? If it did, the driver would be in trouble because this is equivalent to 252 000 kilometres per hour!

Being able to make an **order of magnitude** estimate of a value such as a car's speed helps you to recognise when an answer is not sensible.

What maths skills do you need to make sensible estimates?

1	Knowing if a value is of the right order of magnitude	• Write the value in standard form
		• Make an estimate, to one significant figure in standard form, of the expected value
		• Work out whether the value is sensible by comparing its order of magnitude with the estimate

Maths skills practice

How is estimating useful in checking experimental values?

If you have determined a density value by experiment, you can check if your answer is 'about right' by estimating.

Maths skill 1: Knowing if a number is of the right order of magnitude

The order of magnitude is an approximate measure of the size of a number. If the number is expressed in standard form, the order of magnitude is found by looking at the power to which 10 is raised. For example, the order of magnitude of 2700 is 10^3, because $2700 = 2.7 \times 10^3$. The order of magnitude of 8700 is 10^4, because it is nearer to 10 000 than to 1000.

Practical Investigation 3.1 in the Practical Workbook uses estimation in investigating the acceleration of free fall.

WORKED EXAMPLE 1.8

Experimental determinations of the density of water are:

a $1033 \, \text{kg/m}^3$

b $0.97 \, \text{kg/m}^3$

c $0.095 \, \text{kg/m}^3$

Which one is the correct order of magnitude?

Key question to ask yourself:

Are all of the units the same? To compare orders of magnitude, the values must all be in the same unit.

Yes, they are.

Step 1:   Round the values to one significant figure to make it easier to compare their orders of magnitude.

  a $1000 \, \text{kg/m}^3$

  b $1 \, \text{kg/m}^3$

  c $0.1 \, \text{kg/m}^3$

Step 2:   Consider whether the values are sensible. $1 \, \text{m}^3$ is a large cube with each side $1 \, \text{m}$ long. Considering the likely mass of a volume of water this size, we can conclude that answer A is the only one that makes sense.

Questions

19   Which is the correct order of magnitude for the maximum speed of a cheetah (Figure 1.13)? Circle A, B, C or D.

Figure 1.13: A cheetah.

A $3 \, \text{m/s}$ B $30 \, \text{m/s}$ C $0.3 \, \text{m/s}$ D $300 \, \text{m/s}$

20 The double-decker London bus in Figure 1.14 has a mass of 1.4×10^4 kg.
The area of contact of its tyres with the road is 1490 cm². Estimate the pressure exerted on the road.

Figure 1.14: London bus.

Use the equation pressure $= \dfrac{\text{force}}{\text{area}}$

The force is the weight = mass $\times$ g, and $g = 9.8$ m/s². Give your answer in pascals to 2 s.f.

....

....

....

....

....

....

21

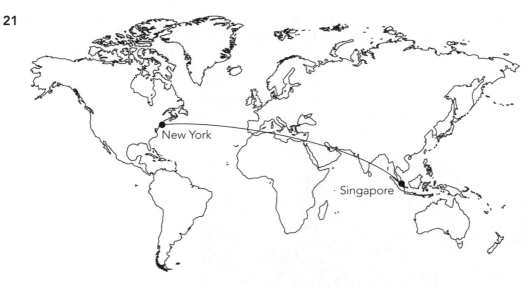

Figure 1.15: Route taken by an aeroplane.

An aeroplane flying at 840 km/hour takes 17 hours 22 minutes to get from New York to Singapore (Figure 1.15). Estimate how far it is in kilometres from New York to Singapore, without using a calculator.

Use the equation: $\text{speed} = \dfrac{\text{distance}}{\text{time}}$

....

....

....

....

....

22 Which row of Table 1.8 gives realistic values for the frequency and speed of the wave type given? Circle A, B, C or D.

	Type of wave	Frequency	Speed in air
A	sound	1.0×10^3 Hz	310 m/s
B	sound	10 Hz	300 mm/s
C	microwaves	1.0×10^{10} kHz	3.0×10^8 m/s
D	microwaves	1.0×10^{-10} Hz	2.9×10^8 km/s

Table 1.8: Which row gives the realistic values?

23 a Calculate the total resistance in the circuit in Figure 1.16.

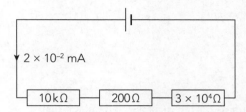

Figure 1.16: Circuit with three resistors.

Give your answer in ohms (Ω) to three significant figures, in standard form.

....

....

....

....

....

b What is the value of the potential difference supplied by the cell? Use the equation for potential difference in terms of current and resistance: $V = IR$

Give your answer to 2 s.f.

....

....

....

....

....

EXAM-STYLE QUESTIONS

1   A tank on the roof of a building is filled with water.

   a   A student uses the equation

$$\text{pressure} = \frac{\text{force}}{\text{area}}$$

to calculate the pressure.

Complete the table to show the correct symbols for the variables and units.   **[3]**

Variable	Symbol for the variable	Name of unit	Symbol for unit
Pressure			
Force			
Area			

The water exerts a force of 2700 kN on the bottom of the tank.

   b   Give the force in standard form.

   ....   **[1]**

   c   The cross-sectional area of the bottom of the tank is 540 000 cm².
       Convert the area from cm² to m².

   [2]

   d   Calculate the pressure. Give your answer in kPa.

Pressure = ... kPa   **[3]**

[Total: 9]

2   Light takes 500 seconds to travel from the sun to the Earth. Light travels at 300 000 kilometres per second.

   a   Give the speed of light in metres per second in standard form.

   [1]

CONTINUED

b Calculate the distance between the Sun and the Earth to three significant figures.

Use the equation: distance = speed × time

Distance = ... km   **[2]**

[Total: 3]

3 It takes 4 hours to recharge a battery fully. The average current supplied by the charger is 300 mA.

Use the equation: charge = current × time

a In the space provided, state this equation using symbols.   **[1]**

b Calculate the amount of charge needed to recharge the battery fully, and give the unit.

Charge = ...   **[3]**

[Total: 4]

COMMAND WORD

State: express in clear terms.

Working with data

Maths focus 1: Understanding and collecting data

As you carry out experiments and record measurements, you are collecting data. These data help you to find and confirm relationships between variables. For example, you can find the speed of sound by measuring the time taken for a sound to travel a measured distance.

What maths skills do you need when collecting data?

1	Identifying types of data	<ul><li>Choose between discrete, continuous or categorical data</li><li>Distinguish qualitative and quantitative data</li><li>Identify the independent variable and the dependent variable</li></ul>
2	Taking measurements	<ul><li>Choose measuring instruments with suitable scales</li><li>Read scales correctly</li><li>Avoid systematic error</li></ul>

Maths skills practice

How does identifying the type of data help with data collection?

KEY WORDS

independent variable: variable in an investigation that is changed by the experimenter

dependent variable: the variable that is measured or observed in an investigation, when the independent variable is changed

control variable: variable that is kept constant in an investigation

---

When planning an experiment, you must be aware of the nature of the data that you will collect. This depends both on the measurement techniques you use and how you categorise information. You need to know which values are the **independent** and **dependent variables**. An independent variable is the one you change in the experiment to test the effects on dependent variables. A dependent variable is what you measure in the experiment. For example, in an experiment to stretch a spring, force/load is the independent variable and extension is the dependent variable. Identifying the independent and dependent variables allows you to know which factor is affecting the other one. Any variable that you have to ensure stays the same throughout an experiment is called a **control variable**.

You also need to understand whether the data are continuous or discrete. For example, when conducting an experiment to see how changing the initial drop height of the ball affects the first bounce height, could you estimate the value of the dependent variable for drop height of 2 metres if you know the first bounce height for 1 metre and 3 metres?

Maths skill 1: Identifying types of data

KEY WORDS

categorical data: data that can be grouped into categories (types) but not ordered

continuous data: data that can take any numerical value within a range

range: the interval between a lowest value and a highest value, for example of a measured variable or on the scale of a measuring instrument

discrete data: data that can take only certain values

There are different types of data:

- **Categorical data** – the data can be sorted into categories (groups) but the categories cannot be easily ordered. For example, the names of materials.

- **Continuous data** – the data can take any value within a certain **range**. For example, the temperature of an object.

- **Discrete data** – where the data can only take certain values. For example, the number of protons in an atom can only be whole numbers.

WORKED EXAMPLE 2.1

You are conducting an experiment to find the critical angle as light emerges into air from semi-circular blocks of different materials. Describe in detail the nature of the data that you will collect and what measuring instrument you will use.

a

b

c
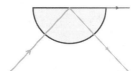

d

Step 1: Start by deciding which variable is the independent variable, and which is the dependent variable.

- The *independent variable* is the one that you choose to change first in an experiment.

- The *dependent variable* is the one that you find the value of, each time the independent variable is changed.

Here, the independent variable is the material of the block, and the dependent variable is the size of the critical angle.

KEY WORDS

quantitative data: data that are numerical

qualitative data: data that are descriptive and not numerical

Step 2: For each variable, decide if it is *qualitative* or *quantitative*. This will tell you how to measure and record it.

- **Quantitative data** – where counting or measurements are taken and recorded as values, for example height in metres.

- **Qualitative data** – where descriptions are recorded, for example names of materials. The type of material is qualitative; the size of critical angle is quantitative – it will be a number.

> **CONTINUED**
>
> **Step 3:** For each variable decide if it is categorical, continuous or discrete.
>
> The type of material is categorical, i.e. a list of names. The critical angle is continuous, i.e. a number that can take any value within a range.
>
> **Step 4:** Decide on which measuring instrument you will use.
>
> As you are finding an angle, you will need to use a protractor.

You can read more about the critical angle of a material in Chapter 13 of the Coursebook.

Questions

1 In an experiment to calculate the speed of sound, Arun and Marcus stand at a fixed distance apart. Arun fires a starter's pistol. Marcus measures the time between seeing the flash of the pistol and hearing the sound. Describe the nature of the data that will be collected and the measuring instruments that will be needed.

....

....

....

....

....

....

2 You are conducting an experiment to find out which factors affect the strength of an electromagnet. You use different core materials but the same number of coils on each. You use an ammeter to measure the current, which is to be kept constant, and you measure the electromagnet's strength using weights, as shown in Figure 2.1.

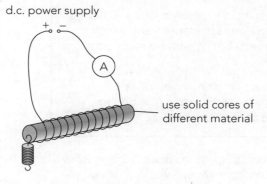

d.c. power supply

use solid cores of different material

Figure 2.1: Measuring the strength of an electromagnet.

Using words chosen from the list provided, describe the data you will collect. You will not need to use all of these words

independent	dependent	discrete	categorical
continuous	qualitative	quantitative	control

....

....

....

Maths skill 2: Taking measurements

Collecting data involves choosing instruments, knowing how to take measurements using them, and recording results accurately.

Make sure that all instruments are zeroed, so that there is no reading when there is nothing being measured. A top-pan balance, for example, must read zero before you add a mass; a ruler may have a gap before the scale as in Figure 2.2. If you do not adjust the reading to zero first, all of your readings will include a **systematic error**.

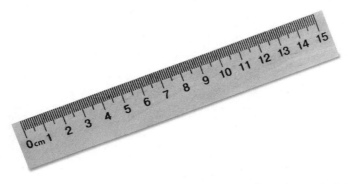

Figure 2.2: The scale on a ruler often starts a few millimetres from the end of the ruler. This must be taken into account.

KEY WORDS

systematic error: measurement error that results in measured values differing from the true value by the same amount each time a measurement is made; this may occur for example when a balance reads 0.02 g with no mass on it

precision: the closeness of agreement between several measured values obtained by repeated measurements; the precision of a single value can be indicated by the number of significant figures given in the number, for example 4.027 has greater precision (is more precise) than 4.0

Choose apparatus that will give you **precise** readings. Look at the pieces of apparatus in Figure 2.3. Which one is most suitable for measuring a liquid volume of 40 cm³? They all have 40 cm³ marked on the surface. The scales on the beaker and the conical flask say 'approx.' so it is better not to use these for measuring. When choosing between measuring cylinders, look for the one that:

- will take the total volume
- has the most 'spread out' scale.

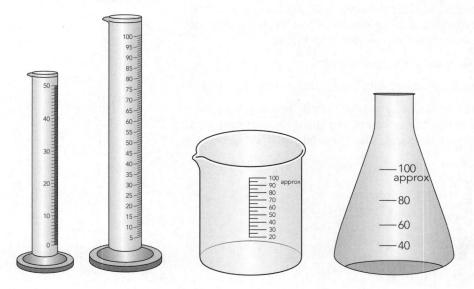

Figure 2.3: Different volume scales.

In this case, both measuring cylinders will hold the full $40\,cm^3$. The smaller measuring cylinder can be read to the nearest $0.5\,cm^3$ but the larger one only to $1\,cm^3$. The smaller one would be the better choice, because the smaller one has the most spread out scale, so the measurements are more precise.

When you read a liquid level or another scale, ensure that your eyes are directly opposite the reading. Otherwise you will introduce what is known as 'parallax error', because you are not looking directly at the reading. Figure 2.4 shows how you can get the wrong reading if your eyes are not in the correct position.

LOOK OUT

Read perpendicular to the scale to avoid parallax error.

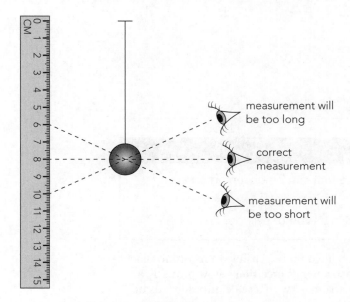

Figure 2.4: Measuring the length of a pendulum bob.

LOOK OUT

Always read at eye level to get an accurate reading.

WORKED EXAMPLE 2.2

A student does an experiment to find whether the density of oil changes with its volume. She uses a measuring cylinder and a top-pan balance. She gradually adds more oil to the cylinder and measures the mass, as shown in Figure 2.5.

Read the instruments shown and record the values in a table.

See Maths focus 2, 'Recording and processing data', for more on drawing tables.

Step 1: Work out how much each space on the scale is worth, by counting how many spaces are between the known values. For example, between the 30 and 40 markers there are 10 spaces. Therefore, one small division is equivalent to $1\,cm^3$.

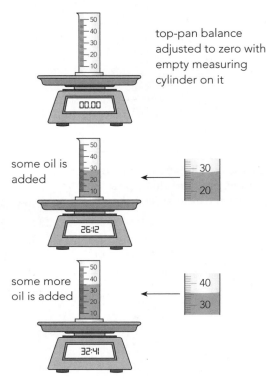

Figure 2.5: Measuring the mass of oil using a top-pan balance.

KEY WORDS

precision: the smallest change in a value that can be observed on a measuring instrument

meniscus: the curved surface of a liquid in a tube or cylinder

Step 2: Decide how many significant figures it would be sensible to record for each instrument. This depends on the instrument's **precision** – how precisely a reading can be evaluated. For an instrument with a scale, this depends on the spacing between the marker lines.

CONTINUED

On the measuring cylinder shown you can read only the whole numbers easily. With care you might be able to read to the nearest $0.5\,\text{cm}^3$.

The digital top-pan balance shows two decimal places, but it is sufficient in this experiment to record the value to just one decimal place – that is, three significant figures for a reading of say $26.1\,\text{g}$. Just one drop of oil could change the second decimal place of the mass reading but would not show on the measuring cylinder.

Step 3: Read and record the level of the bottom of the **meniscus** in the measuring cylinder. Read and record the mass on the top-pan balance (Table 2.1).

	Volume of oil / cm³	Mass of oil / g
First reading	28	26.1
Second reading		

Table 2.1: Recording the mass on the top-pan balance.

Step 4: Record the second set of readings to the same number of significant figures (Table 2.2).

See Chapter 1, Maths focus 3, 'Determining significant figures'.

	Volume of oil / cm³	Mass of oil / g
First reading	28	26.1
Second reading	35	32.4

Table 2.2: Record the second set of readings.

Practical Investigation 1.4 in the Practical Workbook investigates the density of oil using a top-pan balance.

Questions

3   Which of these measuring cylinders has been read correctly? A, B, C or D.

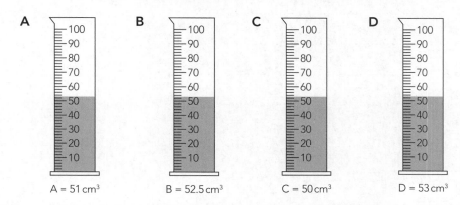

A = 51 cm³   B = 52.5 cm³   C = 50 cm³   D = 53 cm³

4 Figure 2.6 shows two readings from the scale of the same newtonmeter.

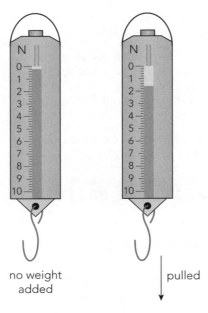

Figure 2.6: Readings on a newtonmeter.

a Describe how you would find the correct value of force reading in the second diagram.

....

....

....

b What is the correct value of the force in the second diagram?

....

c Explain how the experimenter could avoid having to adjust every reading in this way.

....

....

....

....

5 Work out the reading on each of these voltmeters.

a  ....

b  ....

c  ....

d  ....

Maths focus 2: Recording and processing data

When you take readings, you need to record the data. A results table clearly shows your results. Results tables allow you to look for patterns in the figures and to use the data in calculations. Column headings should include the variable name and the units, as shown in Table 2.3.

If the units, such as m/s, include a / sign then it is clearer to allow extra space for the heading and write the units on a separate line, as in Table 2.3. For example, $\dfrac{\text{speed}}{\text{m/s}}$

See Chapter 1, Maths focus 1, Maths skill 1: 'Choosing the correct unit for a variable'.

Distance / m	Time / s	$\dfrac{\text{Speed}}{\text{m/s}}$

Table 2.3: This results table is set up for recording measurements of distance and time and then calculating speed.

What maths skills do you need to record and process data?

1	Designing results tables	• Choose how many columns and rows you will need
		• Ensure that each heading includes the variable name and units
		• Record values in your results table
2	Processing data in tables	• Include extra columns or rows for processing values
		• Use an appropriate number of significant figures in calculated values
		• Include all raw data in the table, as well as processed data

Maths skills practice

How does recording and processing data help you to experiment scientifically?

When carrying out experiments it is important to keep a record of what happens. You need to record all the data in your lab book or notebook. This record may then allow you to determine relationships between the variables. It can also be checked to ensure that:

- the experiment was carried out correctly
- sufficient reliable data was collected
- you have understood how relationships between variables are found.

Maths skill 1: Designing results tables

Tables can be in either of two formats: *vertically* organised or *horizontally* organised, see Figure 2.7.

You also need to include a record of any variable values that you control, for example the value of current in an electrical experiment, if this is kept constant.

Usually the first variable shown in a results table is the independent variable

Length / cm	Current / mA
0	0
10	15

Length / cm	0	10
Current / mA	0	15

Figure 2.7: These tables show the same information but in different formats.

LOOK OUT

It helps to leave space to the right-hand side of a vertical table so that additional columns can be added for processing of the data.

A vertical format allows you to add more columns for repeats of readings if needed. All of the information about a single reading is then on one line and you read across the line much like reading a book. You then look downwards for patterns between different readings.

A horizontal format saves space, but has the disadvantage that the table cannot easily be extended to include more data.

Usually the first variable shown in a results table is the independent variable.

WORKED EXAMPLE 2.3

Designers must ensure that objects they make do not topple over. Buses, chairs, cranes and step ladders all need to be safe from toppling. A student believes that the higher the centre of mass of an object, the easier it will be to topple over. The student uses blocks of wood to build a tower and measures the height of the centre of mass of the tower in millimetres with a metre rule (Figure 2.8). He then tilts the tower and measures the angle at which the structure topples, as additional blocks are added. The highest tower he builds has five blocks.

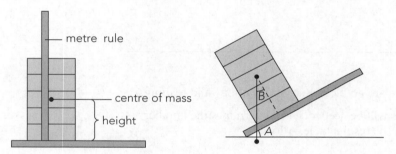

Figure 2.8: Testing a tower of blocks for toppling.

Draw a suitable results table for the experiment.

Step 1: Decide what will be measured and, so, what needs to be recorded in the table.

Key questions to ask yourself:

* What is the *range* of possible readings for the independent variable?

  The range of readings is from the lowest value to the highest value of the variable. There are five blocks, so the range is from the height of the midpoint on one block to the height of the midpoint on five blocks.

CONTINUED

- Which angle, *A* or *B*, will give you the most accurate measure of the angle at which toppling happens?

  It is very difficult to measure angle *A* correctly because the bottom of a protractor has an 'offset' that will produce a systematic error in the results, making each one inaccurate (see Figure 2.9). Although the plumb bob is a piece of string and tends to sway, you can wait for it to settle. Angle *B* will give a more accurate reading.

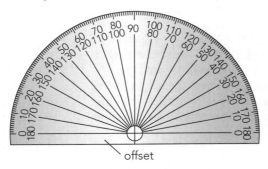

Figure 2.9: The offset of a protractor.

- Is zero blocks a valid reading?

  The 'tower' will not topple if there are no blocks, so zero is not a valid reading.

Step 2: Work out how many readings will be needed. This determines the number of rows below the heading in the results table. Allow:

  - one row: for the headings

  - five rows: one for the height of each set of blocks.

KEY WORD

mean: an average value: the sum of a set of values divided by the number of values in the set

Step 3: Decide if it will be possible to repeat readings and work out a **mean** (average) angle of toppling for each height. This determines the number of columns needed.

  It is easy to repeat readings in this experiment. Allow:

  - one column for the independent variable: height

  - three columns for the dependent variable: actual angle of topple readings

  - one column for **mean** (average) angle of topple.

CONTINUED

Step 4:   Decide on the heading for each column and draw the table.

Height / mm	First angle of topple / °	Second angle of topple / °	Third angle of topple / °	Mean (average) angle of topple / °

Practical Investigation 4.3 in the Practical Workbook investigates the stability of a tower made using blocks of wood.

Questions

6   A student is investigating which of two cans is better at absorbing thermal energy. One can has a shiny surface, the other is painted black (Figure 2.10). The student also has a stopwatch, a thermometer, a measuring cylinder and a radiant thermal source. She fills the cans with water, puts the heater midway between the cans and heats them for 20 minutes.

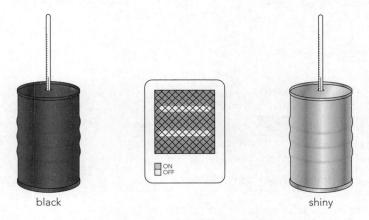

black   shiny

Figure 2.10: Experiment to compare the absorbers of radiation.

a   Draw the results table. Include suitable values for the time readings.

b State why it would be sensible to measure the temperature of the
surroundings while conducting this experiment. Explain your answer.

....

....

7 A student is carrying out an experiment to find out if increasing the number of
turns of wire on an iron C-core affects the strength of an electromagnet. She sets
up the apparatus as shown in Figure 2.11. She uses a hanger with 1 N weights and
an ammeter to ensure that the current through the wire is constant. The insulated
copper wire is long enough to make 20 turns. She tests the strength by measuring
how much force is needed to pull an iron nail away from the core using weights.

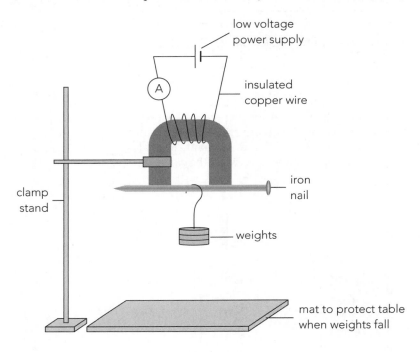

Figure 2.11: Apparatus to measure the strength of an electromagnet.

Prepare a results table for the experiment. Include values for the number of turns
and allow for repeat readings and mean (average) values

Maths skill 2: Processing data in tables

KEY WORDS

raw data: data collected by measurement or observation

processed data: data produced by calculation using raw experimental data

Results tables are used to record the **raw data** (actual measurements) *and* values that are calculated from the data (**processed data**). When recording raw data, you need to decide how many significant figures to record. Any calculated value cannot be more precise than the original raw data.

- When you work out a mean (average), the number of significant figures remains the same as the raw data.

- For other calculated values, look at the raw data you have used and find the value with the lowest number of significant figures. Use that number of significant figures in your calculated figures.

WORKED EXAMPLE 2.4

Eshan uses a 3.0 cm long spring to investigate how the weight on the spring affects the extension of the spring. Each time he adds a 1 N weight to the spring he measures the new length. He repeats the experiment three times, ensuring that the unstretched length remains the same each time. Complete the results table and calculate the mean (average) extension of the spring for each weight.

Weight / N	First length / cm	Second length / cm	Third length / cm	Mean (average) length / cm	Original length / cm	Mean (average) extension / cm
1	4.4	4.5	4.6			
2	5.9	5.8	5.9			
3	7.5	7.4	7.4			
4	9.0	9.2	9.1			

Table 2.2: Results table for Worked example 2.4.

Step 1: Calculate the mean (average) length for each row. Record your answer to the same number of significant figures as the original readings.

The mean (average) value of a set of readings is found in this case from

$$\frac{\text{total of each of the length readings}}{\text{the number of length readings}}$$

CONTINUED

Weight / N	First length / cm	Second length / cm	Third length / cm	Mean (average) length / cm	Original length / cm	Mean (average) extension / cm
1	4.4	4.5	4.6	4.5		
2	5.9	5.8	5.9	5.9		
3	7.5	7.4	7.4	7.4		
4	9.0	9.2	9.1	9.1		

Table 2.3: Results table with completed mean length column for Worked example 2.4

Step 2: Subtract the original length of the spring from each mean length to find the mean extension. The completed table is shown in Table 2.4.

Weight / N	First length / cm	Second length / cm	Third length / cm	Mean (average) length / cm	Original length / cm	Mean (average) extension / cm
1	4.4	4.5	4.6	4.5	3.0	1.5
2	5.9	5.8	5.9	5.9	3.0	2.9
3	7.5	7.4	7.4	7.4	3.0	4.4
4	9.0	9.2	9.1	9.1	3.0	6.1

Table 2.4: Completed table for Worked example 2.4

You can read more about the physics in extension of springs in Chapter 5 of the Coursebook.

Questions

8   Sofia increases the potential difference across an ohmic resistor in 1.0 V steps and for each increase in potential difference measures the current through the resistor. For an ohmic resistor, the current rises evenly for equal rises in potential difference. She conducts the experiment three times. Complete the table and work out the best value for the resistance of the component.

p.d. V / V	First current reading I / A	Second current reading I / A	Third current reading I / A	Mean (average) current reading I / A	Resistance $R = \dfrac{V}{I}$ / Ω
1.0	0.16	0.17	0.17		
2.0	0.34	0.36	0.34		
3.0	0.54	0.55	0.54		

The best value of the resistance is:

....

9   In an experiment to determine the half-life of a radioactive material, the results in the table were obtained. The background radiation was measured at 30 counts/minute. Complete the table to find the values that would be plotted on a graph of net activity against time.

Time / hours	Activity counts/minute	Background count counts/minute	Net activity counts/minute
1	670		
2	340		
3	178		
4	98		
5	65		

10 This experiment tests the conservation of momentum in an 'explosion'. The results are shown in the table. The positive direction of velocity is from left to right in Figure 2.12.

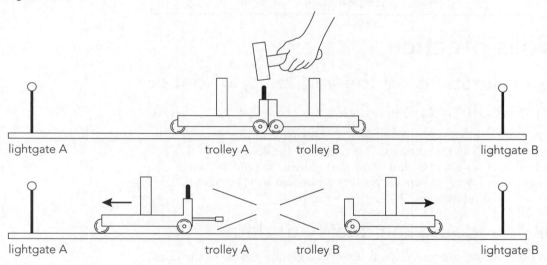

Figure 2.12: Testing the conservation of momentum.

a   Calculate the momentums and find the overall final momentum.

Mass of A kg	Velocity of A m/s	Momentum of A kg m/s	Mass of B kg	Velocity of B m/s	Momentum of B kg m/s	Momentum of A + B kg m/s
0.65	−2.30		0.65	2.40		
0.65	−1.80		0.65	1.70		

b   Comment on the results of the test.

....

....

Maths focus 3: Understanding variability in data

Taking measurements is an inaccurate process. For example, timing with a stopwatch is always affected by reaction time. The results of repeated measurements can be close together in value or spread out. When working with data, you need to know which results to include in your calculations and which can be left out.

What maths skills do you need to be able to understand variability in data?

1	Judging the quality of data	•	Assess the expected uncertainty in measured data
		•	Know the difference between accuracy and precision
		•	Determine whether or not a result is anomalous
		•	Consider possible causes of variability in data

Maths skills practice

How does understanding the variability of data help when calculating half-lives?

When recording the number of counts per minute of a radioactive source material there is a noticeable variability in the readings. This is because the decay rate of a particular sample fluctuates from one instant to the next, due to the random nature of the process of radioactive decay. Whenever possible a physicist will take several readings and work out a mean (average).

Maths skill 1: Judging the quality of data

When you conduct experiments, you need to think about how certain you are of the value of your data point. Is it close to the true value? This is so that you know whether or not the data point is an **anomalous result** that would give rise to an **outlier** on a graph. Identify any anomalies on a graph and exclude these values from **best-fit lines** and calculations.

See Chapter 3, Maths focus 2, 'Plotting the points and drawing a best-fit line'.

KEY WORDS

anomalous result: one of a series of repeated experimental results that is much larger or smaller than the others

best-fit line: a straight line or a smooth curve drawn on a graph that passes through or close to as many as possible of the data points; it represents the best estimate of the relationship between the variables

outlier: a value in a data set, or point on a graph, that is considered unusual compared with the trend of other values

---

KEY WORDS

uncertainty: range of variation in experimental results because of sources of error; the true value is expected to be within this range

random errors: measurement error that varies in an unpredictable way from one measurement to the next

Measurement **uncertainty** leads to variability in repeated results, and depends on:

- the precision of the instrument (for example, 1 V or 1 mV divisions)
- the accuracy of the instrument (for example, whether it has a zero error)
- the nature of what is being measured
- the techniques and skill of the person measuring, which can cause **random errors**.

Whenever you carry out experiments you need to try to reduce random errors. Practising an experiment before taking readings helps. Also taking a mean (average) of repeated results minimises the impact of random error on the values.

KEY WORD

accuracy: how close a value is to the true value

It is important to use the terms **accuracy** and precision in the correct ways. They have different meanings; see Table 2.5.

Accuracy	An *accurate* measurement is close to the true value of the variable.
Precision	• *Precise* measurements are ones for which there is very little spread of repeated measurements about the mean (or average) value; all of the repeated values are near to each other – but not necessarily near to the true value.
	• One way of considering the *precision* of a single measurement is to look at the number of significant figures you are able to state.

Table 2.5: The meanings of accuracy and precision.

WORKED EXAMPLE 2.5

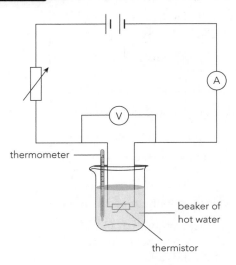

Figure 2.13: Measuring the resistance of a thermistor.

A thermistor is placed in a beaker of hot water and allowed to cool (Figure 2.13). The potential difference across the resistor is kept to 1.0 V by adjusting a variable resistor in the circuit. The resistance is a measure of how hard it is for the potential difference to make a current flow. The current that flows through the resistor is measured and the resistance calculated using

$$\text{resistance} = \frac{\text{potential difference}}{\text{current}}$$

$$R = \frac{V}{I}$$

- The voltmeter has a precision of 0.1 V. This reading is kept constant throughout the experiment.

- The digital ammeter can be read to 0.01 A but the last figure fluctuates as the reading is taken.

- The thermometer has a precision of 0.5 °C but when the temperature is falling rapidly it is only possible to read it to the nearest 1 °C.

- The results from Table 2.6 are plotted on a resistance–temperature graph (Figure 2.14).

CONTINUED

Temperature / °C	Potential difference / V	Current / A	Resistance / Ω
83	1.0	3.85	0.26
80	1.0	3.23	0.31
75	1.0	2.27	0.44
70	1.0	2.00	0.50
60	1.0	1.43	0.70
50	1.0	1.04	0.96
40	1.0	0.77	1.30
30	1.0	0.56	1.80

Table 2.6: Results table for Worked example 2.5

Suggest whether the result for 75 °C is anomalous or is within the expected variation in measurement.

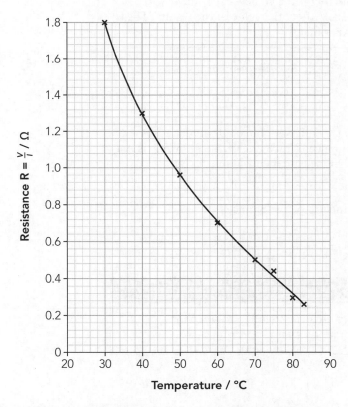

Figure 2.14: Resistance–temperature graph for Worked example 2.5.

CONTINUED

Step 1: Consider the precision of the measuring instruments.

These are 0.1 V, 0.01 A and 0.5 °C.

Step 2: Consider how fast the readings are changing as measurements are taken. The temperature can only be kept constant to within 1 °C while a reading is being taken. The ammeter reading will fluctuate. Try to take the middle value. Does the variation significantly change the reading? In this case it does not.

Step 3: Check that the scale on the graph paper is not so large that the minor variations are overemphasised.

The scale on the graph paper does not overemphasise the readings.

Step 4: Is division involved in the calculation process?

Yes.

Step 5: The value of resistance at temperature 75 °C is anomalous, because the possible variation in values does not significantly affect its position. This means there must be another explanation about the way the reading was taken that has caused the anomaly. For each new experiment you need to think about which factors may affect the value of the results. These factors will be different for each experiment.

Practical Experiment 19.2 in the Practical Workbook investigates thermistors.

Questions

11 In an experiment to measure the height of a ball as it bounces, a student uses a metre rule to measure the height of the bounce. Which one of the following is *not* likely to cause error when taking the height measurement? Circle A, B, C or D.

   A   The ruler is at a slant.

   B   The student's eye was not opposite the top of the bounce.

   C   The speed of the bounce.

   D   The reaction time involved in letting go of the ball.

KEY WORD

rate: a measure of how much one variable changes relative to another variable; usually how quickly a variable changes as time progresses

12 A Geiger counter records the count **rate** of the radioactive isotope technetium-99 as it experiences radioactive decay. The results are shown in Table 2.7.

Time / hours	6	12	18	24	30	36
Count rate counts / minute	250	195	105	56	22	13

Table 2.7: Decay of technetium-99.

A graph of the results is shown in Figure 2.15.

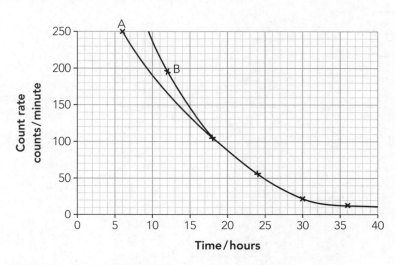

Figure 2.15: Graph of the decay of technetium-99.

Use your knowledge of radioactive decay to decide whether data point A or data point B is an outlier. Suggest a reason for any outlier.

....

....

....

....

....

....

13 A student is carrying out an experiment to find out if heavier athletes take longer to run 100 m than lighter ones. In a trial run of the experiment she asks an athlete of 75 kg mass to run 100 m five times. Between races the athlete was given time to recover. Her results are shown in Table 2.8. What value of time should she take? Explain your reasoning.

	Time / s
1st attempt	8.0
2nd attempt	10.1
3rd attempt	11.1
4th attempt	10.5
5th attempt	11.5

Table 2.8: Results of running a race.

....

....

....

....

....

14 A customer is buying potatoes at a market stall. The stallholder uses a spring balance to find the mass of potatoes. He adds 3 kg of potatoes to the pan of the balance. The customer notices that when the stallholder takes the pan off the balance and is putting the potatoes into the bag, the spring balance records a zero reading. Which statement is correct? Circle A, B, C or D.

A The mass of the potatoes is correct.

B The customer is being given too few potatoes.

C The customer is being given too many potatoes.

D The balance must have been on a slope.

EXAM-STYLE QUESTIONS

1 A student is investigating a circuit containing resistors as shown in Figure 2.16.

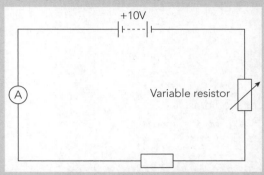

Figure 2.16: Circuit containing a fixed and a variable resistor.

The student wants to find the relationship between the potential difference (p.d.) across the resistor R and the current flowing through R.

a i State the independent variable in this investigation.

.... [1]

ii State the dependent variable in this investigation.

.... [1]

iii Suggest the relationship between the independent and dependent variables stated in parts **i** and **ii**.

.... [1]

b i State the apparatus that you would use to measure the potential difference across R.

.... [1]

ii On the circuit diagram, draw the apparatus connected so that it measures the potential difference across the resistor R.

.... [1]

c The student wants to take five observations.

He records the potential difference readings every 10 mA.

There are two ammeters available in the physics laboratory:

A1: range: 0–50 mA; precision: 1.0 mA

A2: range: 0–50 mA; precision: 0.10 mA

Suggest the ammeter the student should use to measure the current through R.

.... [1]

[Total: 6]

> **COMMAND WORD**
>
> **Suggest:** apply knowledge and understanding to situations where there are a range of valid responses in order to make proposals / put forward considerations

CONTINUED

2   A student investigates the motion of a toy car moving on a flat horizontal surface.

The toy car moves in a straight line.

The student records the distance travelled by the toy car at 2 s intervals.

At time $t = 0$, the distance travelled is $d = 0$.

a   State two measuring instruments the student should use to carry out this investigation.

i   ....

ii   ....   [2]

b   The table shows the measurements.

.... / s	Distance / ....
0	0
	4
	8
	12
	16
	20

i   Complete the column headings in the table.   [1]

ii   Complete the time column in the table.   [1]

[Total: 4]

Chapter 3

Drawing graphs

WHY DO YOU NEED TO DRAW GRAPHS IN PHYSICS?

- Physicists often find it helpful to take data from a results table and display them in a more visual format. The resulting graphs and charts allow any trends in the data to be clearly seen.

- The graph also provides information about the relationship between the dependent and independent variables through the gradient.

- You need to develop graph-drawing skills so that you can do the same in your physics studies.

- Here we will look at drawing line graphs, which have single lines or curves through the data points. These are the most common type of graph needed in physics.

Five key features of line graphs

KEY WORDS

line graph: a graph of one variable against another where the data points fall on or close to a single line, which may be straight, curved, or straight-line segments between points, depending on the relationship between the variables

axis: a reference line on a graph or chart, along which a distance scale represents values of a variable

scale: a set of marks with equal intervals, for example on a graph axis or a measuring cylinder; or, on a scale diagram, the ratio of a length in the diagram to the actual size

best-fit line: straight line or a smooth curve drawn on a graph that passes through or close to as many as possible of the data points; it represents the best estimate of the relationship between the variables

1   Graphs have two **axes** (pronounced ax-ees) drawn at right angles to one another (Figure 3.1). The horizontal axis is called the x-axis. The vertical axis is called the y-axis.

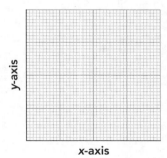

Figure 3.1: Graphs have two axes.

2   Tick marks are evenly spaced along the axes. They have numerical labels to indicate the value of the marked line. This forms a **scale** (Figure 3.2).

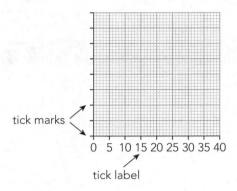

Figure 3.2: Axes have scales.

3   Axis labels are made up of the variable name *and* the unit of the measurement made (Figure 3.3).

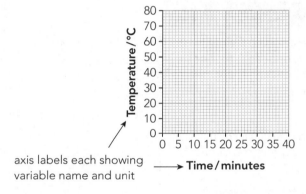

Figure 3.3: Labels on the axes show the variables being measured.

4   Data points are the variable values plotted on the graph, either as small crosses or as dots with small circles around them. Each data point has a pair of values, *x* and *y* (Figure 3.4).

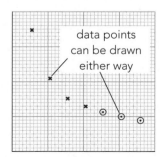

Figure 3.4: Data point are plotted on the graph.

5 If the points show a continuous trend, a smooth **best-fit line** is drawn. This may be a straight line or a smooth curve (Figure 3.5).

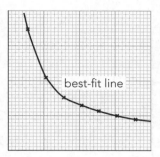

Figure 3.5: Drawing a smooth best-fit line.

The completed graph of temperature against time is shown in Figure 3.6.

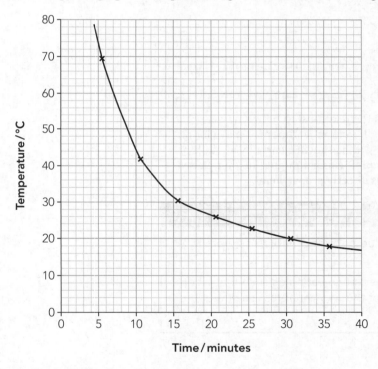

Figure 3.6: Temperature against time graph.

Maths focus 1: Choosing axes and scales

There are *conventions* (accepted rules) about the way graphs are drawn. This avoids confusion in interpretation. Learning the conventions that scientists use will help you to understand everyone's graphs, because they all work in the same way.

What maths skills do you need to choose axes and scales?

1	Choosing which variable goes on each axis	•	Identify the independent and dependent variables in the data
2	Choosing the best axis scales for accuracy	•	Use the range of each variable to plan the scales on the axes
		•	Use as much of the graph paper as you can
		•	Be consistent with the value of each grid square
		•	Avoid scales that make the values hard to read

Maths skills practice

How does choosing axes and scales carefully help you to see a trend in experimental results?

Graphs are used in physics to help us understand the relationship between two *variables*. For example, consider how the current of a circuit component may change as the potential difference across it changes. This will be shown clearly by a graph of the current against potential difference. If the graph forms a straight line that passes through the **origin** (Figure 3.7), the relationship is **directly proportional**.

KEY WORDS

origin: the point on a graph at which the value of both variables is zero and where the axes cross

directly proportional: the relationship between two variables such that when one doubles, the other doubles; the graph of the two variables is a straight line through the origin

---

See Chapter 4 for more on proportions.

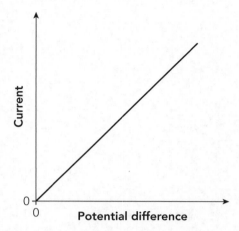

Figure 3.7: A line showing a directly proportional relationship has a constant gradient and goes through the point that is zero on each axis scale. This point is called the origin.

Maths skill 1: Choosing which variable goes on each axis

Start by deciding which variable is the independent one, and which is the dependent one:

- The independent variable is the one that you choose to change first in an experiment.

- The dependent variable is the one that you find the value of, each time the independent variable is changed.

WORKED EXAMPLE 3.1

In an experiment, a student measures the resistance, in ohms (Ω), of a component as its temperature, in degrees Celsius (°C), is changed. Which variable should the student put on each axis?

Step 1: First, read the sentence above very carefully.

Key questions to ask yourself:

- What are the names of the two variables?

  The variables are resistance and temperature.

- Which is the independent variable – the one that you are choosing to change first?

  Temperature is the independent variable – this was chosen to be changed.

- Which is the dependent variable – the one whose values you record as a result of changing the independent variable?

  Resistance is the dependent variable – this was measured when the temperature was changed.

CONTINUED

Step 2: When you have identified which variable is which, allocate them to the correct axes, as shown in Figure 3.8.

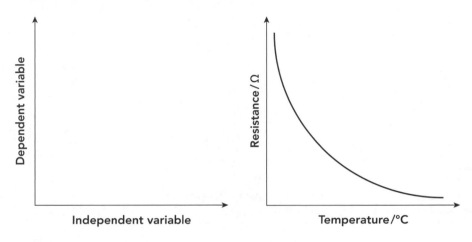

Figure 3.8: Allocating the variables to the correct axes.

The *independent variable* is plotted on the *x*-axis (the horizontal axis).

The *dependent variable* is plotted on the *y*-axis (the vertical axis).

The graph in Worked example 3.1 is called a 'resistance against temperature graph', or a 'resistance–temperature graph'.

If you are asked to draw a graph of 'variable *A* against variable *B*', put *A* on the *y*-axis and *B* on the *x*-axis.

LOOK OUT

If data involves measurements taken as a period of time passes in seconds, minutes, hours, days or years, always plot time on the x-axis. The other variable is the dependent variable and goes on the y-axis.

Questions

1 Zara conducts an experiment to find out how the resistance, in ohms (Ω), of a light-dependent resistor changes when the amount of light it receives decreases. To change the amount of light, she changes the distance from the light source and measures it in metres.

   a Add labels to the axes

b Explain, as if to a friend, how you decided on the label for each axis

....

....

....

....

2 A student keeps a record of the decay of a sample of radioactive material. Each reading is the number of counts on a Geiger counter during a period of 10 seconds. The student takes these readings every 20 minutes for 2 hours.

Graphs A and B in Figure 3.9 both show the results. Decide which one has the axes labelled correctly. Circle **A** or **B**

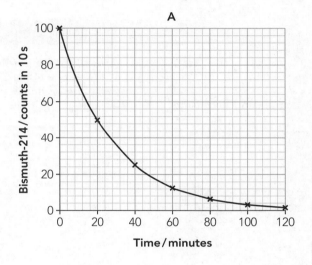 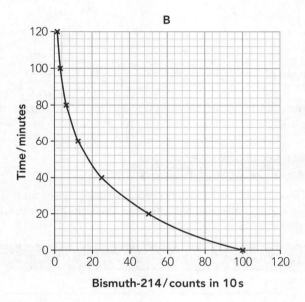

Figure 3.9: Decay graphs of Bismuth-214

When you are sure you have the correct answer, put a cross through the whole of the incorrect graph so that you know it is wrong when you are revising.

Maths skill 2: Choosing the best axis scales for accuracy

To make good quality, accurate graphs you need to spread the data out as much as possible on the graph paper. Show the full data set and choose the scale of each axis so that point plotting and reading off data is straightforward. You may need different scales for each axis.

Use the *range* of each variable to plan the scales on the *x*- and *y*-axes. The range of readings is from the lowest value to the highest value of the variable.

How do you decide what scale to use? Graph paper is like a ruler. The space between the lines is worth the same amount each time. Working out how much this space represents is an important part of preparing a graph (see Figure 3.10).

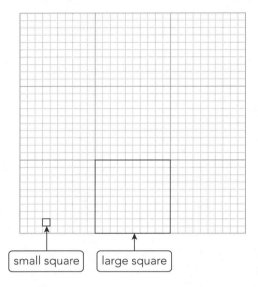

small square   large square

Figure 3.10: Graph paper is divided up into large squares (usually 2 cm square); each large square usually contains five or ten small squares on each side.

WORKED EXAMPLE 3.2

Table 3.1 shows how the speed changes as an aircraft is taking off. Draw the axes for a graph of speed against time. Include the tick marks on each axis and fully label the graph.

Time / s	Speed / m/s
5	15
10	30
15	45
20	60

Table 3.1: Speed measurements for an aircraft taking off.

Step 1: Work out the range of readings in each column.

The range of time is from 5 to 20 s.

The range of speed is from 15 to 60 m/s.

CONTINUED

Step 2: Decide on the scale for the *x*-axis.

Key questions to ask yourself:

• Look at the range of time readings that will be plotted on the *x*-axis. Should the first scale tick on the *x*-axis be zero? If not, what should it be?

  It is sensible to start the axis at zero.

• Consider the main grid lines on the *x*-axis. Which value should the space between the main lines represent: 1, 2, 5, or 10 seconds? Consider marking 0, 1, 2, 3; or 0, 2, 4, 6; or 0, 5, 10, 15; or 0, 10, 20, 30; or 0, 20, 40, 60. Which set of numbers will allow all the data to fill the graph grid provided in the best way?

  In this case it is 0, 10, 20, 30.

Step 3: Now do the same for the *y*-axis. Which set of numbers would make the data fit?

It is sensible to start the axis at zero. In this case the scale 0, 20, 40, 60 would be best (see Figure 3.11).

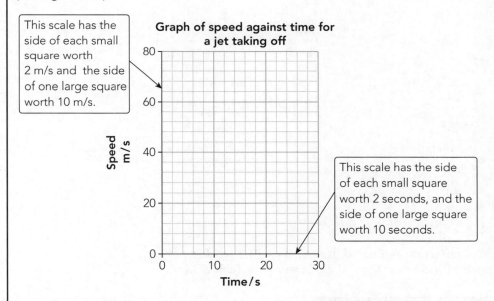

Figure 3.11: Speed–time graph for the jet in Worked example 3.2.

Questions

3 In an experiment, a student heats iced water from 0 °C to become steam at 110 °C. The process takes 12 minutes. The student records the temperature every 2 minutes.

Prepare the axes, tick marks and all of the labels for a graph of temperature against time.

4 A student measures the angle of refraction as a ray of light enters a glass block from the air. They vary the angle of incidence. The results are shown in Table 3.2.

Angle of incidence / °	Angle of refraction / °
80	40
70	38
60	35
50	30
40	25
30	19
20	13

Table 3.2: Measuring the angle of refraction.

Prepare the axes, tick marks and all of the labels for the graph of angle of refraction against angle of incidence.

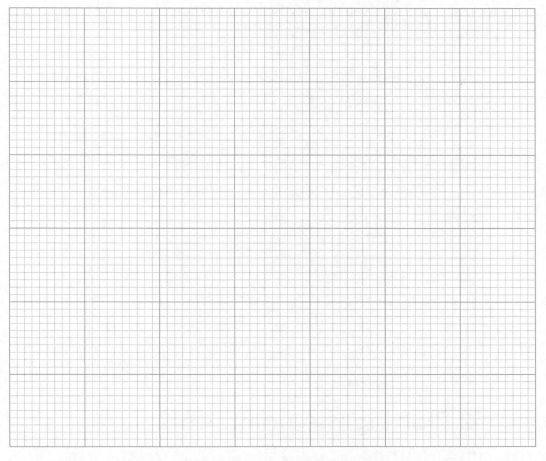

Practical Investigation 13.2 in the Practical Workbook investigates the refractive index of glass by comparing the angle of incidence against the angle of refraction.

5

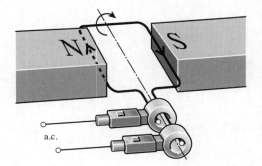

Figure 3.12: A simple a.c. generator.

A student uses an a.c. generator to power a bulb on a bicycle (Figure 3.12). The student records the potential difference every 5 ms for 80 ms. The frequency of the generator is 1 cycle per 20 ms. The maximum value of the potential difference is 4 V. Alternating current (a.c.) generators produce an *alternating* output.

Prepare the axes, tick marks and all of the labels for the graph of potential difference against time.

You will need to include a scale for negative potential difference, as well as positive potential difference. Use the same scale for the positive and negative parts of the graph.

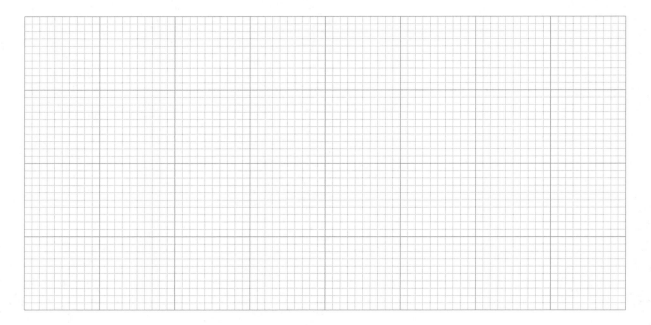

Maths focus 2: Plotting the points and drawing a best-fit line

Plotting data points and drawing a *best-fit line* are skills that help physicists to look at the shape of graphs and interpret them. To make good quality graphs you need to be precise with your point plotting.

What maths skills do you need to plot data points and draw a best-fit line?

1	Plotting points accurately	• Plot points correctly and neatly with a sharp pencil
		• Know how to interpolate between grid lines

2	Drawing a best-fit line	• Decide whether the line should pass through the origin
		• Know that a best-fit line should have roughly the same number of points above it as below it, spread evenly along the line
		• Draw a carefully chosen straight best-fit line using a transparent ruler and sharp pencil
		• Or draw a smooth best-fit curve with one sweeping movement of the hand

Maths skills practice

How does plotting points accurately and drawing a best-fit line help scientific understanding?

Accurately plotted points allow more reliable deductions to be made from graphs. For example, physicists have understood *mass* by conducting accurate experiments and drawing accurate graphs to help them work out equations such as

force = mass × acceleration

$F = ma$

Maths skill 1: Plotting points accurately

The data in a results table give you ordered pairs of readings that can be used for plotting points. In mathematics, ordered pairs are known as **coordinates** and are shown as (x, y). For example, (2, 5).

> KEY WORD
>
> **coordinates:** values that determine the position of a data point on a graph, relative to the axes

Results tables are either shown horizontally or vertically. You need to be able to work with both formats.

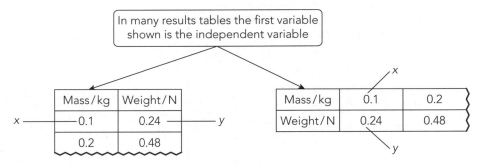

In many results tables the first variable shown is the independent variable

Mass/kg	Weight/N
0.1	0.24
0.2	0.48

x ———0.1   0.24——— y

x

Mass/kg	0.1	0.2
Weight/N	0.24	0.48

y

Figure 3.13: These tables show the same information about the weight of different masses on Jupiter.

The values 0.1 and 0.24 in the tables shown in Figure 3.13 are the first pair of coordinates. These are used to plot the first data point, (0.1, 0.24).

WORKED EXAMPLE 3.3

Arun conducts an experiment investigate whether the mass of honey is directly proportional to its volume. He measures the mass of honey using a scientific balance and the volume with a 100 cm³ measuring cylinder, as in Figure 3.14.

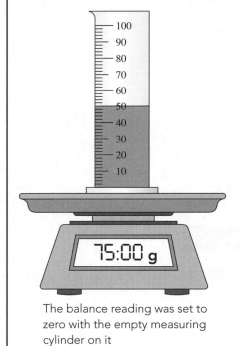

The balance reading was set to zero with the empty measuring cylinder on it

Figure 3.14: Using a balance to meaure mass.

The results are shown in Table 3.3. Plot a graph of mass against volume on the axes given.

Make sure you are correct about which value in the table is x and which is y.

CONTINUED

Volume / cm³	20	30	40	50
Mass / g	30	45	61	75

Table 3.3: Mass of honey for different volumes.

Key questions to ask yourself:

- Will the origin (0, 0) be a data point?

  In this case the origin may be used as a data point because a zero volume has a zero mass. Note that the balance is set to measure the mass of the honey alone, not the honey plus the measuring cylinder.

- What does each space represent on the x-axis?

  On the x-axis of the graph the gap between major grid lines represents a volume of 10 cm³, i.e. every small square represents 1 cm³.

- What does each space represent on the y-axis?

  On the y-axis of the graph the gap between major grid lines represents a mass of 20 g, i.e. every small square represents 2 g.

Step 1: Use your understanding of coordinates to work out where to plot the first point on the grid. The coordinates of the point are (20, 30). See Figure 3.15.

Step 2: To plot a point, first locate its position *on the x-axis*, then find its location *on the y-axis*, and finally look for where these meet.

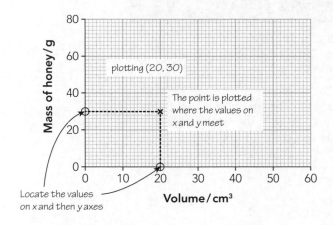

Figure 3.15: Plotting the first point on the grid.

For the first data point the value on the x-axis can be located in the tick marks and is easy to find. Understanding of scale is needed for the y-axis. The major grid lines are marked as 20, 40, 60, 80. There are two ways of finding the line for the value 30, as shown in Figure 3.16.

CONTINUED

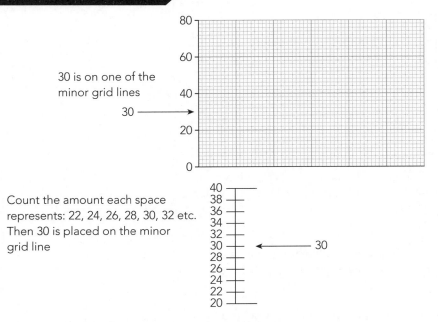

30 is on one of the
minor grid lines

30 ⟶

Count the amount each space
represents: 22, 24, 26, 28, 30, 32 etc.
Then 30 is placed on the minor
grid line

30

Figure 3.16: Two ways of finding the line for the value 30.

Finding the correct grid line for 30

Use a sharp pencil to plot points. Plot each data point with a either a neat
cross or a dot with a small circle round it. The centre of the cross or the
position of the dot marks the exact location of the data point.

KEY WORD

interpolate: on a graph, to estimate the value of a variable from the
value of the other variable, using a best-fit line. On a scale, to estimate a
measurement that falls between two scale marks

Step 3: Plot the remaining data points. Some of the data points will not exactly sit
on a grid line. The y-value of the second data point in the results table is
45 g. You estimate, or **interpolate**, the best position of this between the grid
lines (Figure 3.17).

Count the amount each space
represents: 40, 42, 44, 46, etc.
Then 45 is placed halfway between
the 44 and 46 minor grid lines

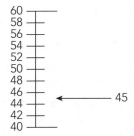

45

Figure 3.17: Interpolating a data point.

CONTINUED

Interpolating between grid lines

All the plotted data points are shown on the graph in Figure 3.18. They appear to be on a straight line through the origin, which means that the mass of honey is *directly proportional* to its volume.

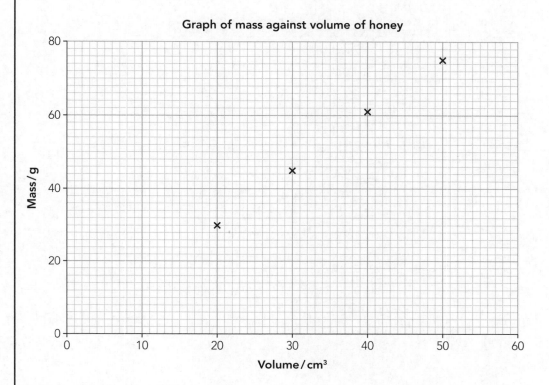

Figure 3.18: Mass against volume graph.

Graphs like this showed physicists the relationship $\text{density} = \frac{m}{v}$

Question

6   A student allows just-boiled water of volume $100\,cm^3$ to cool down and records the temperature. Table 3.4 shows the results for the first 20 minutes.

Plot the data points on the axes given. Note that the temperature scale does not start at zero but at 20 °C (because cooling normally ends at room temperature).

Time / minutes	1	2	3	4	5	6	7	8	9	10	12	14	16	18	20
Temperature / °C	91	82	77	74	71	69	67	65	63	60	59	57	56	54	53

Table 3.4: The temperature of water as it cools down.

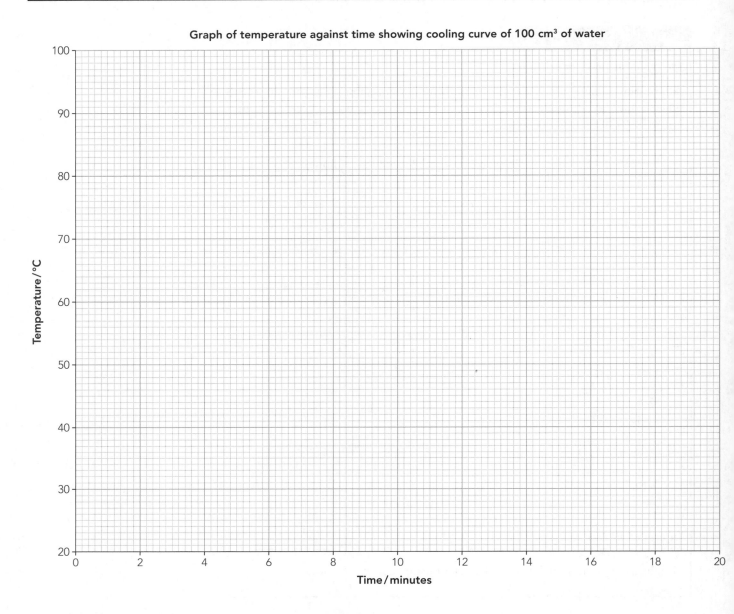

Graph of temperature against time showing cooling curve of 100 cm³ of water

Maths skill 2: Drawing a best-fit line

A best-fit line is a straight line or a smooth curve drawn on a graph that passes
through or as close as possible to the data points. It represents the best estimate of any
relationship between the variables. This means it will be the most accurate line.

WORKED EXAMPLE 3.4

Which graph shows a correctly drawn best-fit line? Circle the correct one.

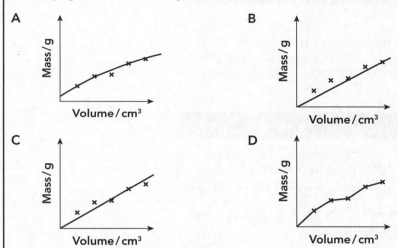

Step 1: Decide if the line/curve should go through the origin (0, 0).

In A, the line does not go through the origin. This is wrong as it shows that material can have mass but no volume.

Step 2: Look at the overall trend of the data points. Decide if they could form a straight line or a curve.

In A, the line has been shown as a curve. This creates a point that appears to be an **outlier**. (Outliers do not fit the pattern. They occur when measurements are taken incorrectly.) This is possible but we can't be sure. A straight line, with several of the points showing a little variation from the line, is more likely.

In D, the line jerks and has been drawn as 'dot to dot'. This shows an inconsistent relationship between variables. *Never* draw a best-fit line like this.

KEY WORD

outlier: a value in a data set, or point on a graph, that is considered unusual compared with the trend of other values

Step 3: Choose the best straight line through the origin. Check to see:

- Are there as many points below the line as above it?

- Are the points that are above and below the line evenly spaced along the line, or bunched at one end?

- Are there any outliers which should have been ignored when drawing a best-fit line?

> CONTINUED

In B, too many data points are above the line. This is not a good estimate of the relationship between the variables.

In C, few data points sit directly on the line but they are all close. In physics, the points plotted have been found by measuring. Measuring always involves inaccuracies. This means that the best-fit line may not always touch the data points, but should be close to them.

> KEY WORD
>
> **trend:** a pattern shown by data; on a graph this may be shown by points following a 'trend line', the best estimate of this being the best-fit line

Graph C shows the best-fit line. It is the best estimate of the **trend** of the data points. In this example none of the points is obviously an outlier.

Circle graph C to help you remember.

Questions

7   From the steps described in Worked example 3.4, create your own checklist of key questions to ask yourself when drawing a best-fit line.

....

....

....

....

....

....

....

8 These graphs show what happens to the pressure when the volume of a fixed mass of gas (kept at a constant temperature) is changed.

a Which curve is the most accurate best-fit line? Circle A, B, C or D.

A

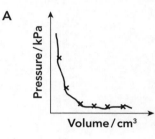

B

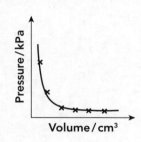

C

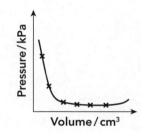

D

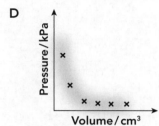

b If you could advise the experimenter to take more readings, which row of Table 3.5 best describes where to take more measurements? Circle A, B, C or D.

	Volume	Pressure
A	more high values	more high values
B	more high values	more low values
C	more low values	more high values
D	more low values	more low values

Table 3.5: Which row best describes where to take more measurements?

Explain your reasoning.

....

....

....

> **LOOK OUT**
>
> If the trend seems to be a straight line, always use a transparent ruler to help you draw the best-fit line.
> Make sure your pencil is sharp.

You can read more about the relationship between the pressure and volume of a gas in Chapter 9 of the Coursebook.

9 A spring is gradually loaded with weights. The extension of the spring is recorded and the graph shown in Figure 3.19 is prepared.

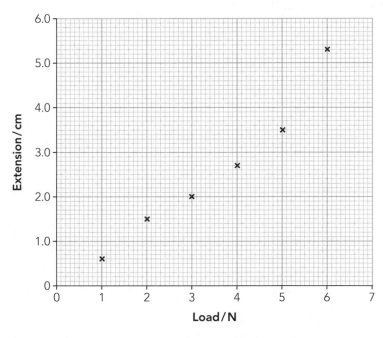

Figure 3.19: Extension against load for a spring.

a Add a best-fit line to the graph. Do you need a ruler to do this?

b Comment on how well the line fits the data.

....

....

10 A student accelerates a 1 kg model truck using a force of 20 N (Figure 3.20). She measures its acceleration with a data logger. She adds additional 1 kg masses to the truck. The force used to accelerate the truck remains the same. She plots the data on the graph shown in Figure 3.21.

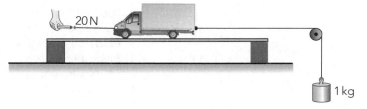

Figure 3.20: Measuring the acceleration of a model truck.

Draw the best-fit curve.

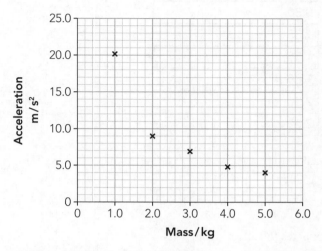

Figure 3.21: Graph of acceleration against mass for the model truck.

11 Marcus measures the time for 20 complete swings of the pendulum using the apparatus shown in Figure 3.22. He repeats the experiment several times by changing the length of the pendulum. Table 3.6 shows the results of the experiment.

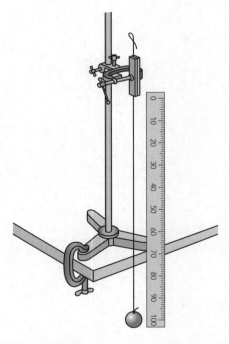

Figure 3.22: Measuring the time period of a pendulum.

Length of pendulum/ m	Time for 20 swings/ s	Mean time for 1 swing/ s
0.20	16	0.80
0.40	25	1.25
0.60	31	1.55
0.80	36	1.80
1.00	40	2.00
1.20	44	2.20

Table 3.6: Results of measuring the time period of a pendulum.

a   Plot the period–length graph for the pendulum.

b   Draw a best-fit curve on your graph.

Practical Investigation 1.3 in the Practical Workbook investigates the effects from changing the length of a pendulum.

12 A student uses an oscilloscope to show the voltage–time trace for a pure sound note. The amplitude of the signal is maximum 0.2 V. The oscilloscope dial shows what each horizontal division on the oscilloscope screen represents.

A student is having difficulty taking measurements from the screen. Draw axes with tick marks and labels to the diagram so that it can be read as a graph.

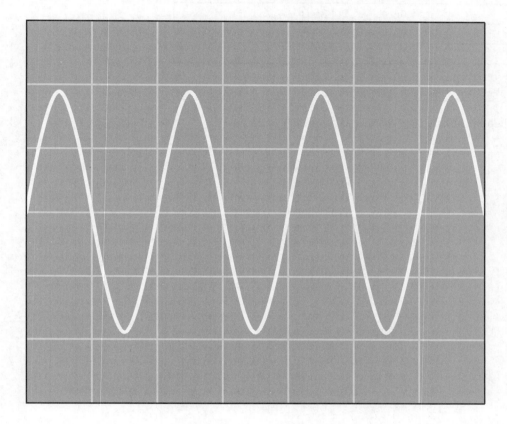

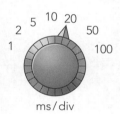

ms / div

13 Table 3.7 shows the orbital velocities of different planets in the Solar System and the distance of the planets from the sun.

Planet name	Distance from the sun / $\times 10^6$ km	Orbital velocity / km/s
Mercury	57.9	47.4
Venus	108.2	35.0
Earth	149.6	29.8
Mars	227.9	24.1

Table 3.7: Orbital velocities of planets in the Solar System.

Plot the graph for the data in the table.

EXAM-STYLE QUESTIONS

1   A student investigates the rate of cooling of hot water. She measures
temperature of the water as it cools down. Table 3.8 shows the results of
the investigation.

t / s	0	30	60	90	120	150
θ / °C	79	65	58	55	53	52

Table 3.8: Results of an investigation into the cooling rate of hot water.

a   Identify which variable goes on the horizontal axis.

.... [1]

b   Identify which variable goes on the vertical axis.

.... [1]

c   Suggest a suitable scale for the *x*-axis and the *y*-axis.

x-axis .... *y*-axis .... [2]

d   Using the results from Table 3.8, draw a graph on the grid provided.   [4]

[Total: 8]

CONTINUED

2 A student uses the circuit shown in Figure 3.23 to determine the resistance of a wire.

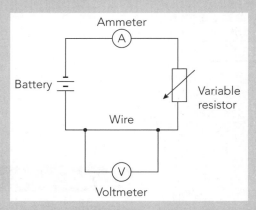

Figure 3.23: Circuit used to determine the resistance of a wire.

The student changes the current through the wire using a variable resistor. She records the potential difference across the ends of the wire for different values of current. The table shows the results.

I / A	V / V	Resistance, $R = \dfrac{V}{I}$ / Ω
1.0	2.0	
2.0	4.0	
3.0	6.0	
4.0	7.8	
5.0	9.6	

a Calculate the resistance for the different values of I and V given in the table. Complete the table.

Use the equation $R = \dfrac{V}{I}$ [1]

[Total: 4]

CONTINUED

b Plot a graph of potential difference against current on the grid. [4]

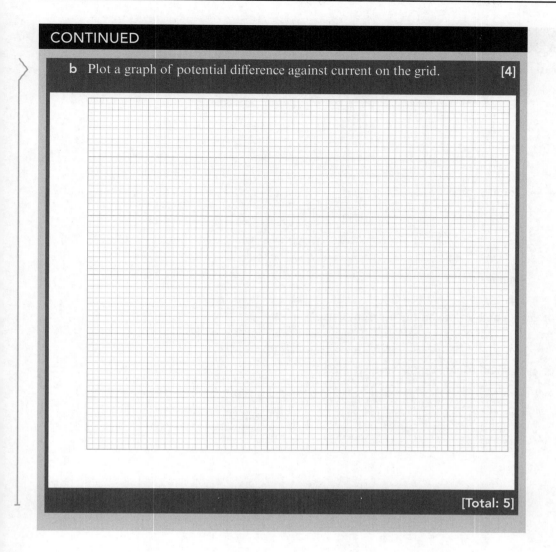

[Total: 5]

CONTINUED

3 The graph shows how to plot the point (20, 30).

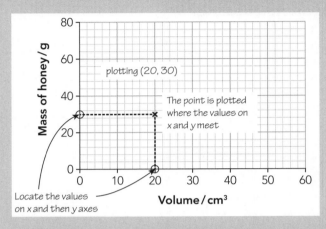

a What is the value of each small square on the horizontal axis?

.... [1]

b What is the value of each small square on the vertical axis?

.... [1]

[Total: 2]

Interpreting data

Four key relationships shown in line graphs

1   **Positive relationship**: As x increases, y increases. The gradient has a positive value (see Figure 4.1).

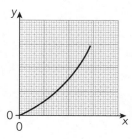

Figure 4.1: A positive relationship.

2   **Negative relationship**: As x increases, y decreases. The gradient has a negative value (see Figure 4.2).

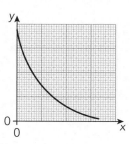

Figure 4.2: A negative relationship.

3   **Directly proportional**: When x is doubled, y doubles; $y = kx$, where k is a constant. The gradient is positive and constant (see Figure 4.3).

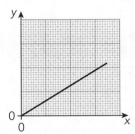

Figure 4.3: A directly proportional relationship.

4   **Inversely proportional**: When x is doubled, y halves; when x is multiplied by 10, y is divided by 10; $y = \dfrac{k}{x}$, where k is a constant (see Figure 4.4).

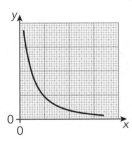

Figure 4.4: An inversely proportional relationship.

Maths focus 1: Reading values from a graph

positive relationship: when one variable increases as the other increases

negative relationship: when one variable decreases as the other increases

directly proportional: the relationship between two variables such that when one doubles, the other doubles; the graph of the two variables is a straight line through the origin

inversely proportional: the relationship between two variables such that when one doubles, the other halves

The ability to extract values from a graph is an important mathematical skill. It helps you to calculate gradients and to work out values that you have not actually recorded in physics experiments. You might have taken readings of temperature every minute and plotted a cooling curve. If you can extract readings from the curve between the plotted points, you can work out what happens at half-minute intervals.

What maths skills do you need to read values from a graph?

1	Interpolating values between known data points	• Read the axes correctly
		• Interpret the coordinates of a point on the graph line
		• Determine the values of the independent and/or dependent variables from a point on the line
2	Extrapolating a graph	• Recognise when a relationship can be assumed to extend beyond the known range
		• Extend the trend line
		• Read values of points on the extrapolated line

Maths skills practice

How does reading values from a graph help in the design of electric circuits?

Electrical components called *thermistors* can be used in circuits to control temperature. These circuits can switch off the current to a heater if the temperature increases too much. Circuit designers can choose a thermistor with a particular resistance range, depending on the switching temperature they require. To do this they can extract values from a calibration graph.

Maths skill 1: Interpolating values between known data points

KEY WORD

interpolate: on a graph, to estimate the value of a variable from the value of the other variable, using a best-fit line. On a scale, to estimate a measurement that falls between two scale marks

One of the reasons for drawing graphs is so that you can estimate values between two known data points. This process is called **interpolating**. It is easier to see the trend on a graph than from a results table, and so the estimate is better. This is especially useful when the values are changing rapidly, such as a rapid fall in the resistance of a thermistor when temperature increases.

WORKED EXAMPLE 4.1

The graph in Figure 4.5 shows the relationship between the temperature and the resistance of a thermistor.

a   What is the value of the resistance when the temperature is 35 °C?

b   Find the temperature when the resistance is 25 kΩ.

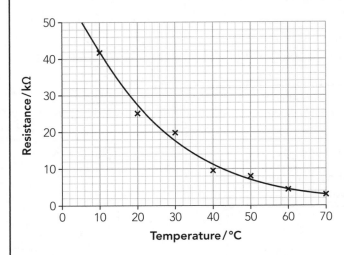

Figure 4.5: Resistance against temperature graph for a thermistor.

Key question to ask yourself:

Does the information in the question have the same units as shown on the graph?

The independent variable (x-axis) is temperature in °C. The dependent variable (y-axis) is resistance in kΩ, so yes, it does.

Step 1:   Identify the known and unknown variables.

Step 2:   For part **a**, find the known value of temperature. Draw a straight line, using a ruler, vertically up to the curve. From here, find the value of the resistance by drawing a horizontal line from the curve to the y-axis (see Figure 4.6).

The value is 14 kΩ.

CONTINUED

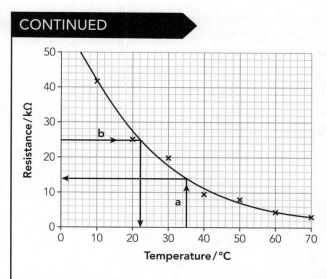

Figure 4.6: Interpolating a graph.

Step 3:   For part **b**, find the 25 kΩ resistance on the *y*-axis. Draw a line from this value horizontally until you reach the curve. From here, find the temperature value by drawing a line vertically downwards to the *x*-axis (see Figure 4.6).

        The temperature is 22 °C.

You can read more about thermistors in Chapter 19 in the Coursebook.

Questions

1   The distance–time graph for runner, Christian Coleman, in a 100 m race is shown in Figure 4.7. Determine the time at which Christian attained a steady speed in the race.

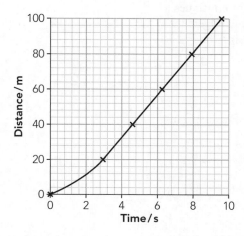

Figure 4.7: Distance–time graph for Christian Coleman in a 100 m race.

Steady speed attained at ....

2 When a 1000 kg car accelerates, its kinetic energy increases as shown in the graph in Figure 4.8. Determine the speed which gives the car a kinetic energy of 70 kJ.

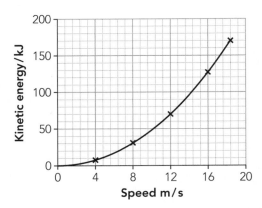

Figure 4.8: Graph of kinetic energy against speed for a car.

Speed at which kinetic energy is 70 kJ = ...

Maths skill 2: Extrapolating a graph

KEY WORD

extrapolate: extending the line of best fit on a graph beyond the range of the data, in order to estimate values not within the data set

In practical work, we often only have time to take a limited number of readings. This can limit the range of readings taken. In order to extend the best-fit line to include extra values, we have to assume that the trend continues in the same way. This is called **extrapolating**. Sometimes extrapolating is sensible: the mass of coins continues increasing when more coins are added. At other times we have to make the judgement that the line cannot continue: Consider the speed of a Formula 1 car passing the finishing flag. The car is likely to slow down.

WORKED EXAMPLE 4.2

Christian Coleman could run 100 m in about 9.6 seconds, and he could also run 200 m in about 19.2 seconds. Imagine he raced 120 m instead of his usual 100 m. Use the graph in Figure 4.9 to predict the time he would take to cover the additional 20 m.

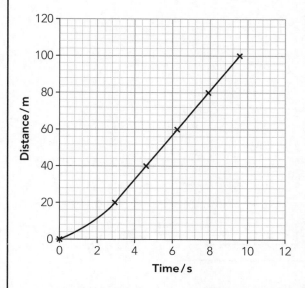

Figure 4.9: Distance–time graph for Christian Coleman with an extended grid.

> **LOOK OUT**
>
> On a distance–time graph, constant speed is shown by a straight line.

Key question to ask yourself:

Is it sensible to extend the straight line on the graph?

In this case, it is, because Christian Coleman could run 20 m at the same average speed that he ran 100 m.

Step 1: Read the labels on the axes to ensure they match the information given in the question.

Step 2: Look at the trend of the graph and, using a ruler, add additional length to the graph line so that 120 metres is reached. Use a dashed line.

Step 3: Find both 120 m and 100 m on the y-axis, as the question asks for *additional* distance. Draw horizontal lines from the values on the y-axis to the graph line.

Step 4: Where these lines meet the graph line or its extension, drop vertical lines downwards to the x-axis (see Figure 4.10).

CONTINUED

Step 5:   Subtract the time value for 120 m from the time value for 100 m:

$$10.7\,s - 9.6\,s = 1.1\,s$$

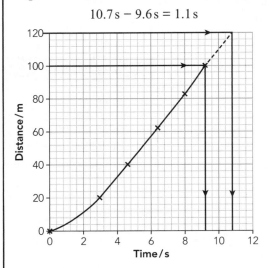

Figure 4.10: Extrapolated distance–time graph for Christian Coleman.

Questions

3   The graph in Figure 4.11 shows how speed in miles per hour (mph) and speed in km/h are converted from one to the other. Use the graph to work out the value in mph of 40 km/h.

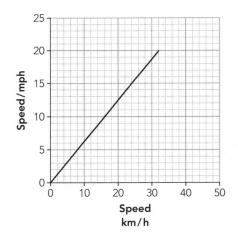

Figure 4.11: A conversion graph for mph and km/h.

....

....

40 km/h = ... mph

4   The graph in Figure 4.12 shows how the pressure (in pascals, Pa) in a container of olive oil increases as the depth of oil is increased. Determine the pressure if the depth is increased to 0.5 m.

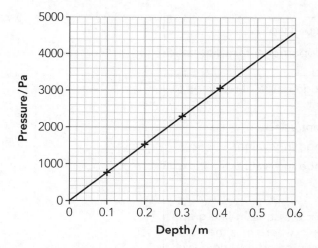

Figure 4.12: Graph of pressure against depth for olive oil.

....

....

Pressure at a depth of 0.5 m = ...

Maths focus 2: Interpreting straight-line graphs

KEY WORD

linear relationship: a relationship between two variables that can be represented on a graph by a straight line.

A straight line on a graph shows that, as the independent variable changes in equal steps, the dependent variable also changes in equal steps. This is called a **linear relationship**.

See Chapter 2 for more on variables.

What maths skills do you need to interpret straight-line graphs?

1	Describing a relationship between variables on a straight-line graph	• Express a relationship in words • Identify a directly proportional relationship
2	Determining the gradient and the intercept	• Choose a wide enough range of readings to determine a gradient • Calculate the gradient using: $$\text{gradient} = \frac{\text{change in } y \text{ value}}{\text{change in } x \text{ value}}$$ or $m = \dfrac{y_2 - y_1}{x_2 - x_1}$ • Write an equation for the straight-line graph in the form $y = mx + c$, where m is the gradient and c is the intercept on the y-axis • Interpret the physical meaning of the gradient and the intercept

Maths skills practice

How does interpreting a straight-line graph help you to write an equation?

An **equation** is a mathematical way of showing a relationship between variables. It is a mathematical statement which includes an '=' sign. Equations make calculating values possible without having to refer to a graph or a results table. For instance, materials scientists use equations derived from graphs of experimental data to predict how materials will behave as the temperature increases. We will look at how they do this in Maths skill 2.

KEY WORD

equation: a mathematical statement, using an '=' sign, showing that two expressions are equal.

Maths skill 1: Describing a relationship between variables on a straight-line graph

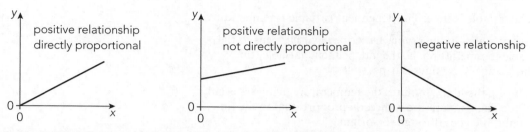

Figure 4.13: Different relationships shown by straight-line graphs.

Relationships shown by straight-line graphs include those in Figure 4.13.

• We show a **positive relationship** by an upward-sloping straight line.

• We show a **negative relationship** by a downward-sloping straight line.

If, and *only if*, the straight line *passes through the origin of the axes* (0, 0), we say that one variable is directly proportional to the other variable. This is a special case of a positive relationship.

Directly proportional means if one variable is doubled, the other variable doubles.

WORKED EXAMPLE 4.3

A solid is heated for 13 minutes. In this time, it changes from solid to liquid and finally becomes a gas. Describe the relationship between the variables shown by the graph in Figure 4.14 for each stage.

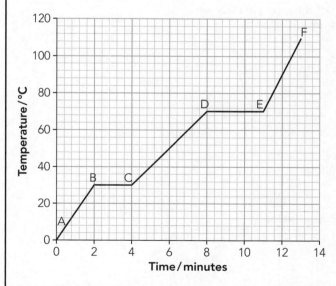

Figure 4.14: Temperature–time graph for a solid being heated.

CONTINUED

Step 1: Read the axes of the graph to establish the independent and dependent variables.

The independent variable is time. The dependent variable is temperature.

Step 2: Identify the distinct stages in the graph. Describe what happens to the dependent variable (temperature), as the independent variable (time) increases, for each stage. Give figures if possible.

From A to B: During the first 2 minutes the temperature increases evenly from 0 °C to 30 °C. The temperature is directly proportional to the time, because the straight line goes through the origin.

From B to C: The temperature stays constant at 30 °C for 2 minutes.

From C to D: The temperature increases evenly from 30 °C to 70 °C. The line is less steep than from A to B, which shows that the rate of increase of temperature with time is now lower.

From D to E: The temperature stays constant at 70 °C for 3 minutes.

From E to F: The temperature increases evenly from 70 °C to 110 °C. This time the rate of increase in temperature is greater, shown by a steeper line.

The relationship is not directly proportional between C and D, nor between E and F, because the extended line does not pass through the origin.

> **LOOK OUT**
>
> A rate of change is a measure of how quickly a variable changes. In this case, it is how much the temperature changes each minute.

Practical Investigation 9.1 in the Practical Workbook investigates changes of state.

Questions

5   The graph in Figure 4.15 shows the distance from Earth of different galaxies plotted against their recession velocity. Describe the relationship shown.

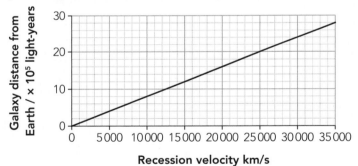

Figure 4.15: Galaxy distance from Earth plotted against recession velocity

....

....

You can read more about galaxies and how they are moving in Chapter 25 of the Coursebook.

6 The pressure of a fixed mass of gas in a container is measured. Which graph in Figure 4.16 shows that the pressure is constant? Circle A, B, C or D.

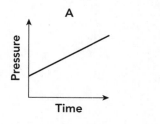 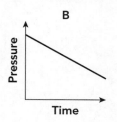 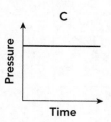 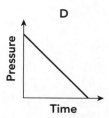

Figure 4.16: Which graph shows constant pressure?

Maths skill 2: Determining the gradient and the intercept

The benefit of straight-line graphs is that they give the evidence for creating a simple equation. All straight-line graphs have the general equation for a straight line

$$y = mx + c$$

where x is the independent variable, y is the dependent variable and m and c are constants (constants are numbers that stay the same).

If the line goes through the origin, then $c = 0$ and the relationship between the variables x and y is directly proportional. Sometimes we say 'y is proportional to x' or write $y \propto x$.

The equation is then

$$y = mx$$

This means that the straight line slopes and goes through the origin.

If the line intersects the y-axis at a point other than the origin, the relationship is not directly proportional (Figure 4.17).

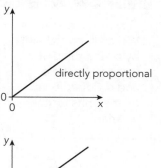
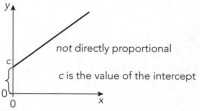
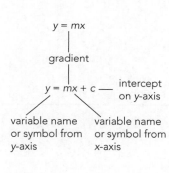

Figure 4.17: Not all straight-line graphs are directly proportional.

If c is non-zero, its value is the value of the **intercept** on the y-axis, where the graph line crosses the y-axis (Figure 4.18).

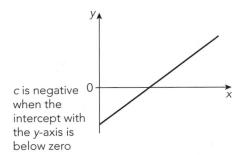

c is negative when the intercept with the y-axis is below zero

Figure 4.18: Sometimes the value of the intercept c can be negative.

The constant m in the equation is the **gradient** of the line. The gradient is the steepness of the line. You can calculate the value of the gradient from

$$\text{gradient} = \frac{\text{change in } y \text{ value}}{\text{change in } x \text{ value}}$$

This shown in Figure 4.19.

$$\text{gradient, } m = \frac{y_2 - y_1}{x_2 - x_1}$$

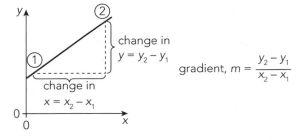

change in $y = y_2 - y_1$

change in $x = x_2 - x_1$

$$\text{gradient, } m = \frac{y_2 - y_1}{x_2 - x_1}$$

Figure 4.19: Calculating the gradient of a straight-line graph.

LOOK OUT

Gradients have units. You can find the units by taking the units for the y-variable and dividing them by the units for the x-variable.

WORKED EXAMPLE 4.4

A spring is stretched by hanging weights from it. The graph in Figure 4.20 shows the total length of the spring as the weights are added.

Describe in words the relationship shown by the graph. Then find the equation for the straight line shown.

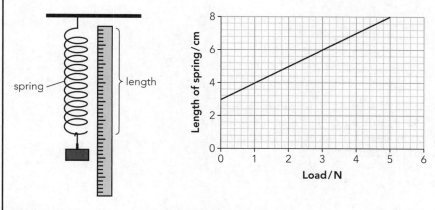

Figure 4.20: Measuring the extension of a spring.

Step 1: Read the axes of the graph to establish the independent and dependent variables.

Independent variable: load
Dependent variable: length of spring

Step 2: Identify what happens to the dependent variable as the independent variable is increased.

The relationship is a straight line, showing that as the load increases the length increases evenly. The equation $y = mx + c$ applies.

Step 3: Determine the value of m. This is the value of the gradient of the line. To calculate an accurate value of the gradient from the graph, you need to choose changes in x and y that cover *at least half* of the straight line (Figure 4.21).

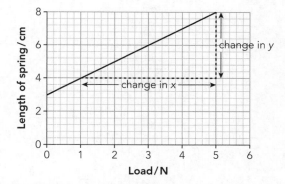

Figure 4.21: Calculating the gradient.

CONTINUED

Use the equation

$$\text{gradient} = \frac{\text{change in } y \text{ value}}{\text{change in } x \text{ value}}$$

$$m = \frac{y_2 - y_1}{x_2 - x_1}$$

$$= \frac{8 - 4}{5 - 1} \, \text{cm/N}$$

$$= \frac{4}{4} \, \text{cm/N}$$

$$= 1 \, \text{cm/N}$$

Step 4: Write down the equation $y = mx + c$ and substitute the values that you know, working from left to right (see Figure 4.22). The load is a force, so we can use *force* as the term for the independent variable. This means we can use the symbols F for force and l for length.

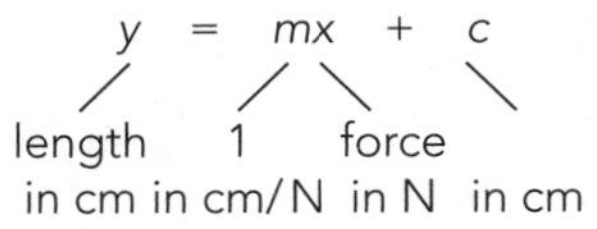

$$y \quad = \quad mx \quad + \quad c$$

length   1   force
in cm   in cm/N   in N   in cm

Figure 4.22: The equation $y = mx + c$.

The equation is

$$l = F + 3$$

where l is in cm and F is in N.

Step 5: Determine the value of c in $y = mx + c$. Look at where the best-fit line hits the y-axis. This is the value of the intercept on the graph.

$$c = 3 \, \text{cm}$$

LOOK OUT

The equation will be different if the variables are in different units. Always specify the units.

Practical Investigation 5.1 in the Practical Workbook investigates the relationship between the extension of a spring and the change in force on a spring.

Questions

7   The circuit in Figure 4.23 is used to measure how the current through a resistor changes as the potential difference across it is increased.

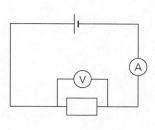

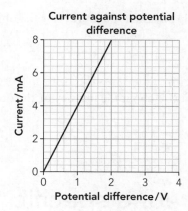

The resulting graph is shown.

Figure 4.23: Circuit for measuring current through a resistor and graph of the results.

a   Find the gradient. State the unit.

....

....

....

b   Find the intercept.

....

c   Write the equation that shows the relationship between current (symbol I) in mA and potential difference (symbol V) in V.

....

8   Figure 4.24 shows a distance against time graph for a moving object.

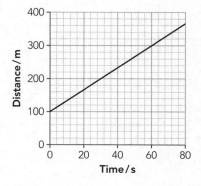

Figure 4.24: Distance–time graph.

a Find the values of the gradient and the intercept for this line. Then write the equation that represents the line. Use the symbols d for distance (in m) and t for time (in s).

....

b What does the value of the gradient tell you about the journey of the object?

....

....

c What does the value of the intercept tell you about the journey of the object?

....

....

Maths focus 3: Interpreting specific types of linear graphs

KEY WORD

intersect: where two lines on a graph meet or cross one another

There are some specific graphs which need careful interpretation, for example when a graph shows two events happening. The graph has two lines and these may **intersect** (meet) and possibly cross over one another.

What maths skills do you need to interpret specific types of linear graph?

1	Interpreting the intersection of lines on a graph	•	Identify the values on the x-and y-axis where the lines intersect
		•	Relate the intersection to the physical context
2	Calculating the distance travelled from a speed–time graph	•	Identify the difference between a speed–time graph and a distance–time graph
		•	Calculate the areas of rectangles and triangles under a graph line

Maths skills practice

How do intersections on a graph give us additional information?

In a 4000 m race, one runner is likely to overtake another. At the point of overtaking, the runners are in the same place at the same time. The intersection between the lines on the distance–time graph shows the overtaking (Figure 4.25). If the runners have started together from the same position, the distance they have run is the same at this intersection.

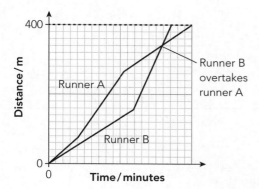

Figure 4.25: The intersection on the graph shows that one runner overtook the other, and where and when this happened.

Maths skill 1: Interpreting the intersection of lines on a graph

WORKED EXAMPLE 4.5

The total energy of a falling object is made up of gravitational energy (GPE) and kinetic energy (KE). The graph in Figure 4.26 shows the energy values when the object is at different heights.

At what height is the KE value equal to the GPE value, and what is this value?

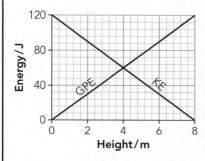

Figure 4.26: Graph of energy against height for a falling object.

CONTINUED

Step 1: Identify the dependent and independent variables.

Independent variable: height
Dependent variable: energy

One line represents gravitational energy (GPE). The other line represents kinetic energy (KE).

Step 2: Find the value of the independent variable for the intersection.

The intersection happens at height of 4.0 m.

Step 3: Find the value of the dependent variable for the intersection.

The value of both types of energy at 4.0 m, the intersection, is 60 J.

Note that this is half the total energy and happens at half the maximum height.

Questions

9   Railway engineers are designing a new straight route between two towns, A and B. It is cheaper to create a passing place for trains going in opposite directions, than to lay two tracks. The passing place will be at a new station where the trains will stop.

The distance–time graph in Figure 4.27 shows the planned motion of two non-stop trains. The distance is measured from station A. Train P is the outward going train. Train Q is another train on the return journey.

a   Determine how far from station A the new station should be, so that the trains can pass each other there.

....

b   On this graph, which train, P or Q, has the greater speed? How do you know? Discuss with your classmates.

....

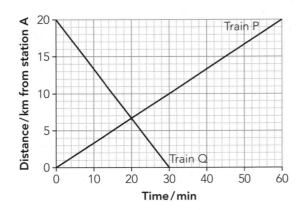

Figure 4.27: Distance–time graph for two trains.

10 A student compares the behaviour of some materials when an increasing load is used to stretch them. The graph of her results shows the extension of a piece of strong elastic and the extension of a metal spring, for different loads (Figure 4.28). Both are the same length at the start of the experiment.

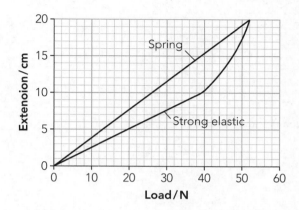

Figure 4.28: Graph of extension against load for two materials.

Determine the load for which they again have the same length

They have the same length at a load of ....

Maths skill 2: Calculating the distance travelled from a speed–time graph

From a speed–time graph, you can find the distance travelled by calculating the area under the graph line. This works because the area represents speed × time, which equals the distance.

WORKED EXAMPLE 4.6

The graph in Figure 4.29 shows how the speed of a runner changes with time.

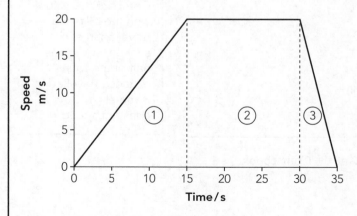

Figure 4.29: Speed–time graph for a runner.

Which statement about distance is correct?

A   The runner travels further while accelerating than at constant speed.

B   The runner travels 200 m altogether.

C   The runner travels 80 m when accelerating.

D   Over half of the total distance is run at constant speed.

Step 1:   Split the graph into sections 1, 2 and 3, as shown.

Step 2:   Work out the area under the graph in section 1 between 0 and 15 seconds.

Area under the line = area of the triangle

∴   distance travelled $= \frac{1}{2} \times$ base $\times$ height

$= \frac{1}{2} \times 15\,\text{s} \times 20\,\text{m/s}$

$= 150\,\text{m}$

Step 3:   Work out the area under the graph in section 2 between 15 and 30 seconds.

Area under the line = area of a rectangle

distance travelled = width $\times$ height

$= 15\,\text{s} \times 20\,\text{m/s}$

$= 300\,\text{m}$

Step 4:   Work out the area under the graph in section 3 between 30 and 35 seconds.

Area under the line = area of the triangle

distance travelled $= \frac{1}{2} \times$ base $\times$ height

$= \frac{1}{2} \times 5\,\text{s} \times 20\,\text{m/s}$

$= 50\,\text{m}$

Step 5:   Find the total distance travelled.

Total distance = 150 m + 300 m + 50 m

$= 500\,\text{m}$

Half the total distance is $\frac{1}{2}$ of 500 m = 250 m

Therefore statement D is correct.

LOOK OUT

Compare this value with the distance travelled in each section – over one half of the total distance travelled is run at constant speed.

You can read more about speed–time graphs in Chapter 2 of the Coursebook.

Questions

11

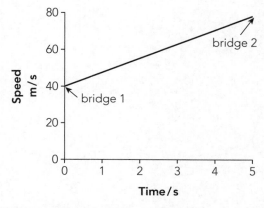

Figure 4.30: Speed–time graph for a train.

A train passes under a bridge at a speed of 40 m/s and then accelerates along a straight track to another bridge. Use the information from the graph in Figure 4.30 to determine the distance between the two bridges.

....

....

LOOK OUT

The area under the line must be the whole area right down to the time axis. This forms a trapezium. The area of a trapezium can be found by creating a rectangle and a triangle. You may remember the formula for the area of a trapezium from Maths.

12 A bus leaves a bus stop and accelerates uniformly (at a constant rate) for 20 s over a distance of 100 m. Using information from the graph in Figure 4.31, calculate the final speed of the bus.

The speed axis in Figure 4.31 has no values, but the question gives information about the starting speed.

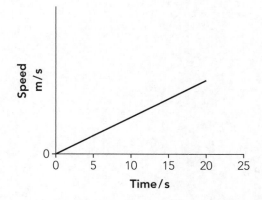

Figure 4.31: Speed–time graph for a bus.

....

....

13 A manufacturer makes central heating radiators to standard length and heights (Figure 4.32). Table 4.1 shows the power output of a series of *double panel* radiators of height 750 mm.

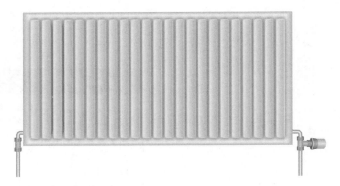

Figure 4.32: A radiator.

Length of radiator / m	0.6	0.9	1.2	1.5	1.8
Power output / W	1600	2400	3200	4000	4800

Table 4.1: Power output of radiators.

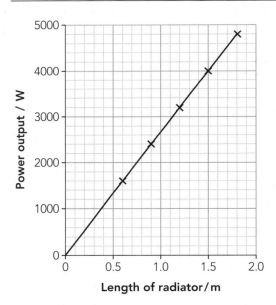

a Determine the equation for the relationship shown by the graph.

....

b From the graph, find out what the power output of a radiator that is 0.5 m long would be.

....

c On the graph, sketch the relationship between power output and length that you would expect for a *single panel* radiator.

Maths focus 4: Interpreting curves on graphs

You need to be able to interpret some graphs that curve, for example a graph of continuously changing speed on a distance–time graph.

What maths skills do you need to interpret curves on graphs?

1	Extracting data from a curve on a graph	•	Read values from the graph
		•	Interpret changing gradients
		•	Relate the information from the graph to the physical context
2	Determining when a relationship is inversely proportional	•	Calculate reciprocal values of x, i.e. $\frac{1}{x}$
		•	Replot the data as y against $\frac{1}{x}$
		•	Identify whether the new graph forms a straight line
3	Interpreting graphs with regularly repeating patterns	•	Identify and calculate the amplitude and frequency of the graph
		•	Relate the information from the graph to the physical context

Maths skills practice

How does interpreting a curved graph help us to describe complex relationships?

Complex trends in data can be interpreted, linked to real-life situations, and used to develop theories. For example, the speed of a parachutist can be recorded during the fall, and plotted against time. Looking at the changing shape of the curve, and explaining what is happening to the gradient and the dependent variable (speed) as the independent variable (time) is changing, is a way to help physicists describe behaviour and test theories.

Maths skill 1: Extracting data from a curve on a graph

A description of how the gradient of a curve is changing gives important information. For instance, on a speed–time graph, this tells us how the acceleration is changing, whether it is getting greater, smaller or staying the same.

Table 4.2 summarises some characteristics of motion graphs.

Graph	Gradient is equal to	Meaning of a downward sloping line	Meaning of a horizontal line	Area under graph is equal to
distance–time graph	speed	returning towards start position	no change in distance, i.e. stationary	—
speed–time graph	acceleration	decelerating, i.e. slowing down	no change in speed, i.e. moving at constant speed; if the line is along the x-axis the object has stopped	distance travelled

Table 4.2: Summary of motion graphs.

WORKED EXAMPLE 4.7

A parachutist jumps from a hot air balloon and free falls. The graph in Figure 4.33 shows her speed against time. She pulls her parachute open after 28 seconds.

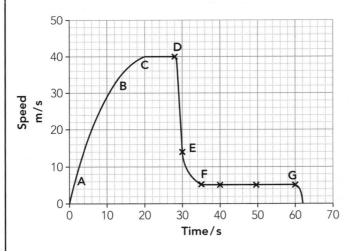

Figure 4.33: Speed–time graph for a parachutist.

a   Describe in words what happens to the speed and the acceleration at each of the points **A** to **G** on the graph.

CONTINUED

b   Where on the graph is a negative relationship shown?

c   For how long was the parachutist travelling at 5 m/s?

d   Calculate the acceleration when the change in speed was greatest.

Key question to ask yourself:

When a graph line changes, what new description/calculation is needed?

This depends on the physical context. Think about this carefully.

a   At **A**, the parachutist starts to fall. Her speed increases: she *accelerates*.
At **B**, the speed is still increasing but more slowly. The *acceleration is lower*.
At **C**, the speed reaches its maximum value and stays the same until **D**.
This constant speed is called *terminal velocity*. The *acceleration is zero*.
At **D**, the speed decreases rapidly. This is a *high deceleration*.
At **E**, the speed is decreasing more slowly. The *deceleration is lower*.
At **F**, the parachutist reaches a new *lower constant speed* (a new terminal velocity). The *acceleration is zero*.
At **G**, the parachutist lands, slowing down rapidly to a stop.
The *deceleration is large*.

b   A negative relationship is one where there is a *downward sloping line*. As the values on the *x*-axis increase, the values on the *y*-axis fall. This happens from **D** → **E** → **F** and from **G** onwards.

c   25 seconds (from 35 s to 60 s)

d   The change of speed is greatest between **D** and **E**, where the line is steepest.

Acceleration = gradient of the speed–time graph

$$= \frac{14 - 40 \, \text{m/s}}{2 \, \text{s}}$$

$$= \frac{-26}{2} \, \text{m/s}^2$$

$$= -13 \, \text{m/s}^2$$

The negative sign shows deceleration: the parachutist is slowing down.

Questions

14 Match the following descriptions to the velocity–time graphs in Figure 4.34.

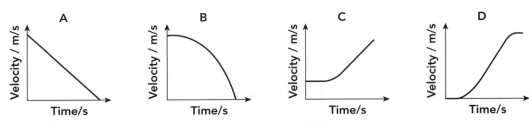

Figure 4.34: Four velocity–time graphs.

    i   A car braking hard. The fastest change of speed happens at the end of the braking.

        Graph ....

    ii   A parked car accelerates to a constant speed.

        Graph ....

    iii   A motor cycle braking with uniform deceleration.

        Graph ....

    iv   A rocket travelling at constant speed fires its second burner, causing acceleration.

        Graph ....

15 The characteristic curve of current against potential difference for a filament lamp is shown on the graph.

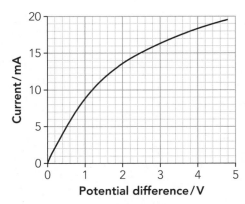

    a   Mark on the graph, with the letter A, the region where the filament lamp has low resistance. Low resistance happens when a small change in potential difference produces a high change in current.

    b   Mark on the graph, with the letter B, the region where the lamp's resistance is highest.

Maths skill 2: Determining when a relationship is inversely proportional

When a graph shows a downward curve (Figure 4.35), it is worth checking whether the relationship is inversely proportional. This inversely proportional relationship is in the form

$$y = \frac{k}{x}$$

where k is a constant.

We say that y is inversely proportional to x or write $y \propto \frac{1}{x}$. When x doubles, y halves; or when x increases to $5x$, y decreases to $\frac{y}{5}$.

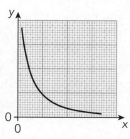

Figure 4.35: Graph curve showing an inversely proportional relationship.

If we plot y against $\frac{1}{x}$, and the best-fit line is a straight line through the origin (Figure 4.36), this shows that y is inversely proportional to x.

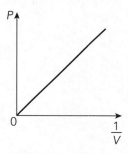

Figure 4.36: This graph shows that when the temperature is kept constant, P is inversely proportional to V, so $P = k\left(\frac{1}{V}\right)$ or $P = \frac{k}{V}$.

WORKED EXAMPLE 4.8

A hammer is used to hit a variety of nails with a force of 200 N. The nails are all exactly the same, apart from the size of the head. The experimenter has calculated the pressure exerted on the nail head and recorded the results in Table 4.3. Find the relationship between the pressure and the area.

Force / N	Area of nail head / mm²	Pressure / N/mm²	Reciprocal area / $\frac{1}{mm^2}$
200	1	200.0	1.00
200	2	100.0	0.50
200	3	66.7	0.33
200	4	50.0	0.25
200	6	33.3	0.17
200	8	25.0	0.13
200	10	20.0	0.10

Table 4.3: Results table.

Step 1: Plot a graph of pressure against area (Figure 4.37).

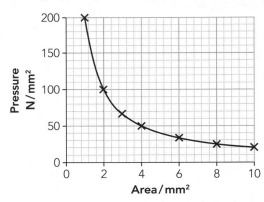

Figure 4.37: Pressure against area.

Step 2: This looks as if it might be an **inversely proportional** relationship. Check by calculating the reciprocal of the area values (the right-hand column in Table 4.3).

CONTINUED

Step 3: Plot a graph of pressure against $\frac{1}{area}$ (Figure 4.38).

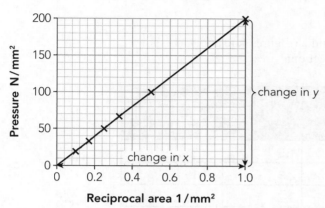

Figure 4.38: Pressure against $\frac{1}{area}$.

Step 4: The graph is a straight line going through the origin, so the relationship between pressure and area is confirmed as being inversely proportional.

$$\text{Pressure} = \frac{k}{area}, \text{ or pressure} = k\left(\frac{1}{area}\right)$$

Step 5: Calculate k, which is the gradient of the straight-line graph.

$$\text{Gradient, } k = \frac{\text{change in } y}{\text{change in } x}$$

$$k = \frac{200 - 0}{1.0 - 0\,\text{N}}$$

$$k = 200\,\text{N}$$

Step 6: Substitute this into the equation to find the relationship.

$$\text{Pressure} = \frac{200}{area}$$

where pressure is in N/mm² and area is in mm².

Questions

16 A student used the circuit in Figure 4.39 to measure the resistance of 1 m lengths of wire of the same material but different cross-sectional area.

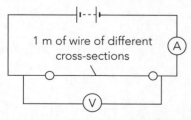

Figure 4.39: Circuit to measure the resistance of wire.

For each piece of wire the students measured the potential difference across the wire and the current. The student repeated the experiment three times and calculated the resistance of each piece of wire using the equation

$$\text{resistance} = \frac{\text{mean potential difference}}{\text{mean current}}$$

The results are shown in Table 4.4. Graphs 1 and 2 (Figures 4.40 and 4.41) show the relationship between resistance and cross-sectional area.

Cross-sectional area of wire / mm²	Mean potential difference / V	Mean current / A	Resistance / Ω	Reciprocal cross-sectional area / 1 mm²
0.16	0.69	0.460	1.5	6.3
0.11	0.72	0.313	2.3	9.1
0.08	0.77	0.241	3.2	12.5
0.06	0.85	0.193	4.4	16.7
0.04	0.93	0.141	6.6	25.0
0.03	1.15	0.134	8.6	33.3

Table 4.4: Results table for Question 16.

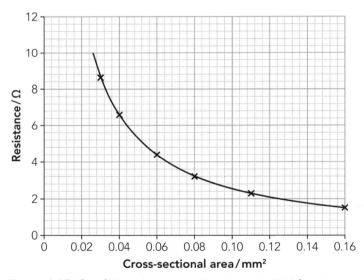

Figure 4.40: Graph 1: resistance against cross-sectional area.

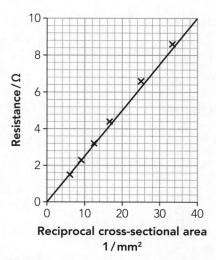

Figure 4.41: Graph 2: resistance against reciprocal cross-sectional area.

a Complete these sentences using the words *increases* and *decreases*.

From Graph 1: As the cross-sectional area ...., the resistance

of the wire ....

From Graph 2: As $\dfrac{1}{\text{cross-sectional area}}$ ...., the resistance

of the wire ....

b Do these graphs give you sufficient evidence to say that the resistance is inversely proportional to the cross sectional area? Explain your reasoning.

....

....

c Determine the mathematical relationship between resistance and cross-sectional area for 1 m of this type of wire.

....

....

17 Figure 4.42 shows four motion graphs for a car. Which graph shows that the car's acceleration slowly increases until a steady speed is reached?
Circle A, B, C or D.

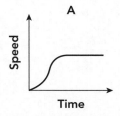
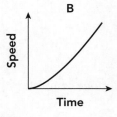
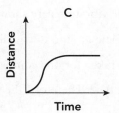
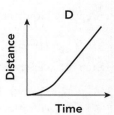

Figure 4.42: Motion graphs for car.

Maths skill 3: Interpreting graphs with regularly repeating patterns

Many events involve repeated movements: the orbits of the planets, the rotation of a bicycle wheel, vibrations and waves. These give graphs with curves that repeat regularly as time passes. Physicists need to extract useful data from these graphs, so that they can try to explain the physical cause of the shape of the curves.

WORKED EXAMPLE 4.9

The graph in Figure 4.43 shows the movement of an air particle as a sound wave passes.

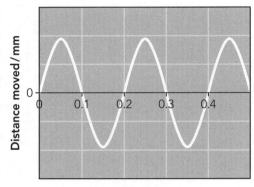

Figure 4.43: Distance against time for an air particle.

Determine the frequency of the wave, and mark the amplitude of the motion on the graph.

Key question to ask yourself:

How do you distinguish between wave frequency and amplitude?

Frequency is about how often the wave vibrates, that is, the number of complete vibrations in one second.

Amplitude is about the amount of energy put into each vibration, that is, the size of the vibration from the central line to the peak.

Step 1: Determine the position of the air particle when there is no wave passing.

It would be on the x-axis.

Step 2: How many complete vibrations are shown?

There are two complete up-and-down vibrations.

Step 3: Determine the time taken for one complete vibration.

Two vibrations take 0.4 s. Therefore, the time taken for one complete vibration is 0.2 s.

CONTINUED

Step 4: Calculate the frequency, i.e. the number of vibrations that happen in one second.

As one vibration takes 0.2 s, there are $\frac{1}{0.2}$ in 1 second. So the frequency is 5 vibrations per second or 5 Hz.

Step 5: Mark the amplitude (see Figure 4.44). This is the maximum distance moved by the air particle above (or below) the zero line.

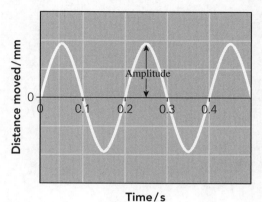

Figure 4.44: Marking the amplitude.

Questions

18 A tidal stream generator is used on the coast to generate electricity from moving seawater. The graph shows how the height of the tide varies over time, above and below a mean. Use the graph to answer the following.

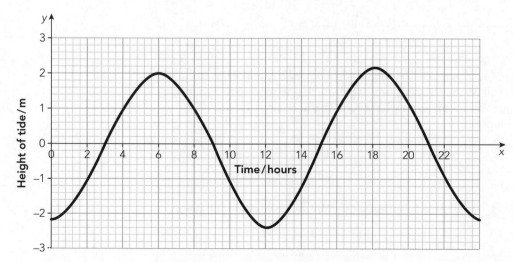

a   What is the maximum height of the tide above the mean?

....

CAMBRIDGE IGCSE™ PHYSICS: MATHS SKILLS WORKBOOK

b How far below the mean is the lowest tide?

....

c On a falling tide, label a point F when is the height is changing fastest. This is when more electricity can be generated.

d Label a point S on the graph when the height is changing most slowly.

19 The graph in Figure 4.45 shows the daily temperature variations of the outside air and of the inside of two different buildings in a city on the Equator.

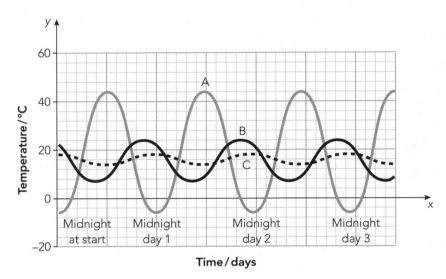

Figure 4.45: Daily temperature variations inside and outside building on the Equator.

a State which graph line represents the outside air temperature. Explain your reasoning.

....

....

b A building made of a material with a high thermal capacity can delay and limit the rise and fall of the temperature. State which line represents the inside of a building made from a material with a high thermal capacity. Explain your reasoning.

....

....

c Determine the difference between the maximum and the minimum outside air temperature.

....

....

Maths focus 5: Interpreting data in other types of chart/diagrams

What maths skills do you need to be able to interpret data in other types of chart/diagram?

1	Interpreting pie charts	• Read and calculate values from the chart
		• Relate the information from the chart to the physical context
2	Interpreting bar charts	• Determine the vertical scale
		• Read and calculate values from the chart
		• Relate the information from the chart to the physical context
3	Interpreting Sankey diagrams	• Read and calculate values from the Sankey diagram
		• Relate the information from the diagram to the physical contex

Maths skills practice

How does being able to interpret different types of chart help in physics?

> **KEY WORDS**
>
> **pie charts:** a circular chart that is divided into sectors which represent the relative values of components; the angle of the sector is proportional to the value of the component
>
> **bar charts:** a chart with separated rectangular bars of equal width; the height (or length) of a bar represents the value of the variable
>
> **Sankey diagram:** a diagram that shows all the energy transfers taking place in an energy transfer process; the thickness of the arrow determines the amount of energy involved

Data can be presented in many different ways. Physicists interpret the data and link the information to their current knowledge, in order to further their understanding. In addition to line graphs, in your studies you may come across **pie charts**, **bar charts** and **Sankey diagrams**.

Maths skill 1: Interpreting pie charts

Pie charts are circular charts with sectors, used to show how a total amount is split into portions (normally percentages). The size of the sector angle is proportional to the value the sector represents. For example, in electricity production, the percentages of the total produced from coal, gas, nuclear, renewables, oil and other sources are shown in the pie chart in Figure 4.46. This type of chart is good for comparison, but actual values may not be shown.

WORKED EXAMPLE 4.10 ⟩

The pie chart in Figure 4.46 shows the percentages of China's electricity generated from different sources in 2020. Calculate the percentage of China's electricity that was generated from gas.

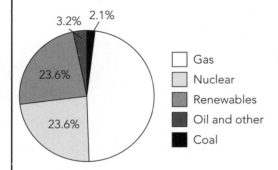

☐ Gas
▨ Nuclear
▨ Renewables
▨ Oil and other
■ Coal

Figure 4.46: Percentages of China's electricity generated from different sources in 2020.

Step 1: Add up the percentages shown for the other energy sources.

$$2.1 + 3.2 + 23.6 + 23.6 = 52.5$$

Step 2: Subtract this from 100.

$$100 - 52.5 = 47.5$$

47.5% of China's energy was generated from gas.

See Chapter 1, Maths focus 4, 'Representing very large and very small values'.

Question

20 The total amount of electricity generated in China in the first three months of 2020 was 75.5 TWh (1 TWh = 10^9 kWh. TWh are beyond the requirements of the syllabus).

Using the data in the pie chart in Figure 4.46, determine how much electricity was produced during this three months from gas and from renewables.

Give your answers to 3 s.f.

i Electricity from gas = ...

ii Electricity from renewables = ...

Maths skill 2: Interpreting bar charts

Bar charts show, by the height of a bar, the size of a variable for different categories. They provide a visual comparison.

WORKED EXAMPLE 4.11

Worked example 4.10 shows that renewable energy sources produced approximately 30% of China's total electricity supply in 2020. The bar chart in Figure 4.47 shows the amounts contributed to this by different types of renewable energy source (1 TWh = 10^9 kWh).

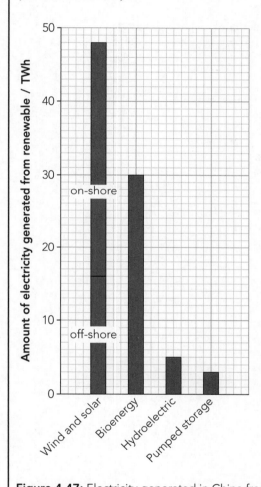

Figure 4.47: Electricity generated in China from different types of renewable source in 2020.

Use the information to find the total electrical energy generated in 2020. Give your answer to 3 s.f.

See Chapter 1, Maths focus 3, for more on significant figures.

CONTINUED

Step 1: Read the values for each source from the graph.

Wind and solar: 48 TWh, of which off-shore is 16 TWh and on-shore 32 TWh
Bioenergy: 30 TWh
Hydroelectric: 5 TWh
Pumped storage: 3 TWh

Step 2: Find the total from all renewable sources.

$$48 + 30 + 5 + 3 = 86 \, \text{TWh}$$

Step 3: 86 TWh is 30% of the total energy generated and you need to calculate 100%. Divide 86 by 30 to find 1%, then multiply by 100 to find 100%.

$$\text{Total energy generated} = \frac{86}{30} \times 100 = 287 \, \text{TWh}$$

Practice question

21 The bar chart in Figure 4.48 shows the densities of different materials.

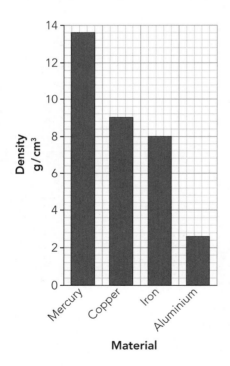

Figure 4.48: Densities of different materials.

Use the values shown on the graph to calculate the mass of 350 cm³ of each material. Use the equation

$$\text{density} \left(\text{in } \frac{g}{cm^3}\right) = \frac{\text{mass (in g)}}{\text{volume (in cm}^3)}$$

Give your answer to 3 s.f.

....

....

....

Maths skill 3: Interpreting Sankey diagrams

Sankey diagrams show all the energy transformations taking place in an energy transfer process. The thickness of the arrow determines the amount of energy involved. The larger the width of an arrow, the larger the energy transfer. In a Sankey diagram, the input is from the left of the diagram, the useful output is to the right and wasted output is made to go up or down. For example, the Sankey diagram in Figure 4.49 shows that 85 J of energy is wasted as thermal energy and only 15 J is the useful energy.

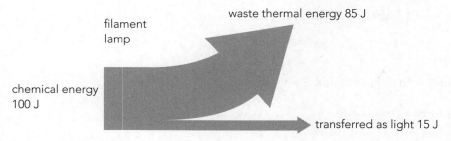

Figure 4.49: Sankey diagram for a filament lamp.

WORKED EXAMPLE 4.12

A solar cell transfers chemical energy from the Sun as electricity and into thermal energy.

Figure 4.50: Sankey diagram for a solar cell.

The Sankey diagram in Figure 4.50 shows what happens to each 100 J of energy that is used by a solar cell. Using the diagram, calculate the efficiency of the solar cell using the equation

$$\text{efficiency} = \frac{\text{useful energy output}}{\text{total energy input}} \, 100\%$$

> CONTINUED

Key questions to ask yourself:

- Which part of the diagram shows the total input energy?

  The left of the diagram shows the input energy.

  Input energy = 100 J

- Which energy is the useful energy?

  The arrow to the right shows the useful energy.

  Useful output energy = 60 J

- Which energy is the wasted energy?

  The arrow going down shows the wasted energy.

  Wasted energy = 40 J

  $$\text{efficiency} = \frac{\text{useful energy output}}{\text{total energy input}} \times 100\% = \frac{60\,\text{J}}{100\,\text{J}} \times 100\% = 60\%$$

You can read more about Sankey diagrams in Chapter 6 of the Coursebook.

Questions

22 Figure 4.51 shows the Sankey diagram for an electric motor. Using this Sankey diagram, calculate:

70 J

100 J

useful energy

Figure 4.51: Sankey diagram for an electric motor.

a the useful amount of energy

....

....

b the efficiency of the electric motor, using the equation

$$\text{efficiency} = \frac{\text{useful energy output}}{\text{total energy input}} \times 100\%$$

....

....

23   Figure 4.52 shows the Sankey diagram for a coal-fired steam locomotive that is supplied with 3400 J of energy. How much energy is wasted?

3400 J

600 J

Figure 4.52: Sankey diagram for a coal-fired locomotive.

24   The Sankey diagram in Figure 4.53 is for a 20 W lamp turned on for 10 seconds. Find the mistake in the diagram

200 J

150 J

150 J

Figure 4.53: Sankey diagram for a lamp.

....

....

EXAM-STYLE QUESTIONS

1 A trolley is released from the top of an inclined plane. A student is investigating how the distance moved by the trolley depends on the angle the inclined plane makes with the floor.

The graph in Figure 4.54 shows the results obtained.

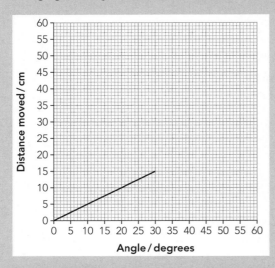

Figure 4.54: Distance moved by a trolley for different angles of inclination.

a Describe the relationship between distance moved and the angle using the graph.

....

.... [2]

b State the equation to calculate value of the gradient of the graph.

.... [1]

c Calculate the gradient of the above graph using your answer to part **b**. State the unit.

....

....

....

Gradient = ... unit .... = [3]

d Using the graph, predict the distance moved by the trolley when the plane is inclined at an angle of 50°.

....

.... [2]

[Total: 8]

COMMAND WORDS

Describe: state the points of a topic / give characteristics and main features

Predict: suggest what may happen based on available information

CONTINUED

2 In a cooling experiment, a student records the change in temperature
   of a beaker of hot water with time.

   The graph in Figure 4.55 shows the relationship between temperature and time.

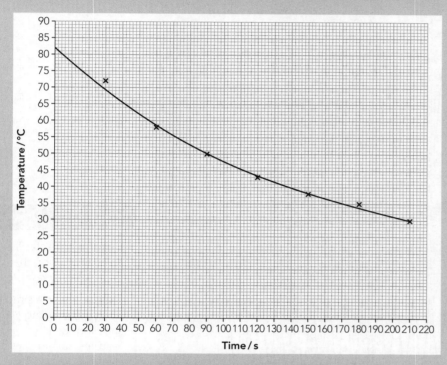

Figure 4.55: Temperature changes in hot water as it cools.

a Give the temperature of the water at 90 seconds.

   .... [1]

b State whether there is a difference in the rate of cooling of water
   between first 50 seconds of the experiment and the last 50 seconds
   of the experiment.

   .... [1]

c Justify your answer in part **b** using the graph.

   ....

   .... [2]

COMMAND WORD

Justify: support a
case with evidence/
argument

CONTINUED

3 The graphs in Figure 4.56 show the waveforms for two different sounds A and B.

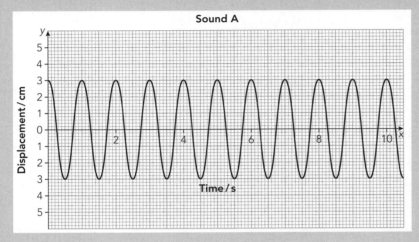

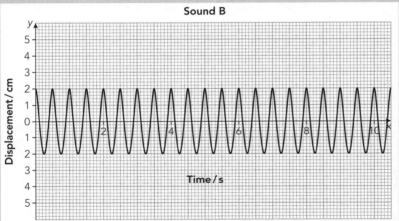

Figure 4.56: Waveforms of two sounds, A and B.

COMMAND WORDS

Determine: establish an answer using the information available

Sketch: make a simple freehand drawing showing the key features, taking care over proportions

a The maximum displacement above (or below) the x-axis shows the amplitude of the sound wave.

Determine the amplitude of

i sound A .... [1]

ii sound B .... [1]

b The greater the amplitude of the sound wave, the louder the sound.

Which sound is louder ? Circle the correct one.

Sound A **Sound B** [1]

c Sketch another sound wave which is two times louder than that for sound B on the graph for sound A. [2]

[Total: 5]

CONTINUED

4   The graph in Figure 4.57 shows how the speed of a car changes with time.

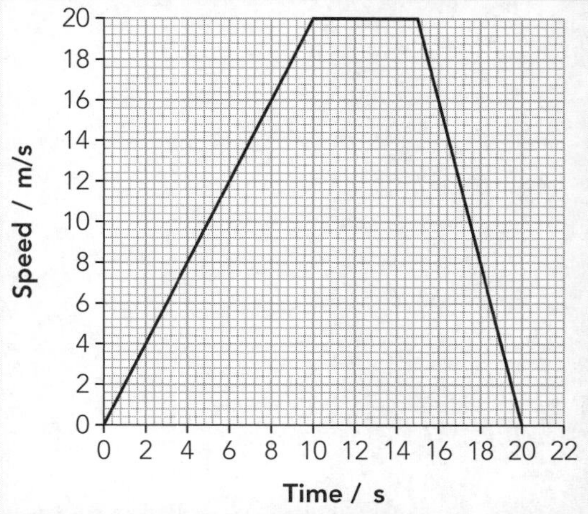

Figure 4.57: Speed–time graph for a car.

a   State the maximum speed of the car ....   [1]

b   State how long it took to reach the maximum speed ....   [1]

c   Calculate the acceleration of the car in first 10 seconds.

....

....

....

....

Acceleration = ... unit ....   [4]

d   Deduce the total distance travelled by the car during the journey.

....

....

....

....

....

Distance = ... unit ....   [5]

[Total: 11]

COMMAND WORD

Deduce: conclude from available information

CONTINUED

5 The Sankey diagram in Figure 4.58 shows the energy transfers taking place in a generator.

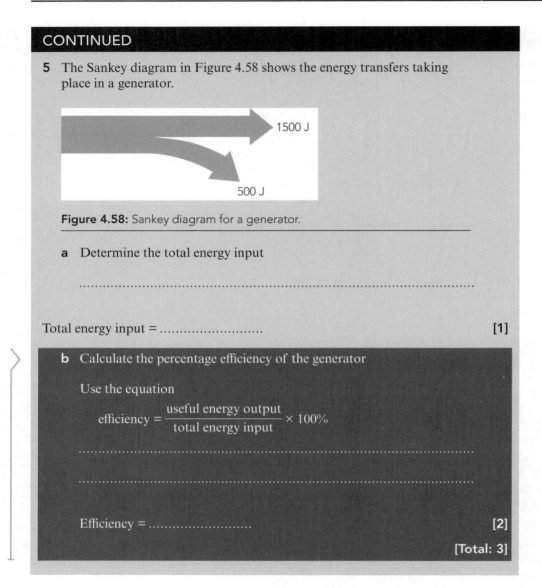

1500 J

500 J

Figure 4.58: Sankey diagram for a generator.

a Determine the total energy input

....

Total energy input = ... [1]

b Calculate the percentage efficiency of the generator

Use the equation

$$\text{efficiency} = \frac{\text{useful energy output}}{\text{total energy input}} \times 100\%$$

....

....

Efficiency = ... [2]

[Total: 3]

Chapter 5

Doing calculations

WHY DO YOU NEED TO DO CALCULATIONS IN PHYSICS?

- Equations in physics are mathematical descriptions of relationships between real quantities.
- The equations allow us to calculate unknown values by using mathematical procedures.
- Physicists use equations to calculate values that they would otherwise have to measure through observation. It is much simpler to use an equation.
- We can also use equations to check that measurements have been made accurately.

Maths focus 1: Understanding equations

KEY WORD

equation: a mathematical statement, using an '=' sign, showing that two expressions are equal; an equation that shows the relationship between variables

Equations are a mathematical way of showing relationships between variables. They are often used to define a variable. For example, the equation $W = mg$ shows how multiplying the mass of an object m by g, the gravitational field strength, gives the weight W of an object.

What maths skills do you need to understand equations?

1	Working with equations: the basics	• Know that equations express relationships
		• Understand the = sign
		• List the quantities given
		• Substitute values and units correctly into equations
2	Calculating with percentages	• Change fractions to percentages
		• Change percentages to fractions

Maths skills practice

How does understanding an equation help you to solve problems in physics?

Solving physics problems written in words needs some skill, as you need to choose the correct equation to work with. If you want to find speed from information about distance and time, you need to choose the equation

$$\text{speed} = \frac{\text{distance}}{\text{time}}$$

and then substitute the known values correctly into the equation. Putting the values in incorrect places can give you completely the wrong answer for speed. If you understand the relationship that the equation is describing, you are less likely to make errors.

Maths skill 1: Working with equations: the basics

What is the importance of the symbol '='? The equals sign means 'the same as'. It shows that both sides of an equation have the same value *and* equivalent units.

This means that if you change one side of an equation in any way, the other side of the equation needs to be changed in the same way.

The simplest way to show this is to use an example with numbers:

$3 + 4 = 7$

Now we add 2 to both sides:

$3 + 4 + 2 = 7 + 2$

If we had added 2 to only one side, then the equation would no longer be true.

If you understand the equals sign in this way, then you will see that the sides of an equation can be swapped over. For example, look at the transformer equation which shows you how the number of turns on the primary and secondary coils affect the way potential differences are stepped (changed) up or stepped (changed) down.

N_p and N_s are the number of turns on the primary and secondary coils.

V_p and V_s are the potential differences across the primary and secondary coils.

The equation is

$$\frac{N_p}{N_s} = \frac{V_p}{V_s}$$

With the left and right sides swapped over, this becomes

$$\frac{V_p}{V_s} = \frac{N_p}{N_s}$$

An unknown V_p now becomes much easier to calculate, because it is on the left-hand side of the equation at the top. You now just need to multiply both sides by V_s to find the value of V_p.

> **LOOK OUT**
>
> Remember that whatever we do to one side of an equation, we must do exactly the same to the other side of the equation to maintain the equality.

KEY WORD

rearrange: to manipulate an equation mathematically so that the unknown value can be calculated; also termed 'change the subject'

This swapping over is useful when you want to **rearrange** an equation, for example to make what is on the top line of the right-hand side appear on the top line of the left-hand side. We will consider this in Maths focus 2.

WORKED EXAMPLE 5.1

Find the weight of an object of mass 700 g when it experiences a gravitational field strength of 7.0 N/kg.

Step 1: Make a list of the variables in the question and their values with units.

$$W = ?$$
$$m = 700\,g$$
$$g = 7.0\,N/kg$$

Step 2: Convert any inconsistent units. The gravitational field strength is N/kg, so the mass needs to be in kilograms.

$$700\,g = 0.7\,kg$$

See Chapter 1 for more on variable symbols and units.

Step 3: Choose the equation that you need. *Make sure that there is only one unknown value*, because it not possible to work out answers using one equation when there are two unknowns. Write down the equation.

$$W = mg$$

Step 4: Substitute the values and units into the equation.

$$W = mg$$
$$W = 0.7\,kg \times 7.0\,N/kg$$

Step 5: Calculate the unknown value, remembering to include the unit.

$$W = 4.9\,N$$

Questions

1   Zara stands 165 m away from a cliff face and shouts. She hears the echo after 1.0 s.
Calculate the speed of the sound.

....

....

....

2 A solid rectangular object has sides 2 cm, 2 cm and 4 cm. Its mass is 320 g.

a Find the density of the object.

....

....

....

b State whether the object will float or sink in water. The density of water = 1 g/cm³.

....

3 A train travelling at 15 m/s has a mass of 6000 kg.

a What is the value of its kinetic energy? Give your answer in standard form to 2 s.f.

See Chapter 1, Maths focus 3, 'Determining significant figures' for more on significant figures.

....

....

....

b The speed is doubled. What is the new value of its kinetic energy? Give your answer in standard form to 2 s.f.

....

....

Maths skill 2: Calculating with percentages

KEY WORD
percentage: a fraction expressed out of 100, e.g. $\dfrac{1}{2} = \dfrac{50}{100} = 50\%$

Percentages are very useful for comparing values. 'Per cent' means 'out of a hundred', so 38% means $\dfrac{38}{100}$ or 0.38.

- To change a % to a fraction, write the value as a fraction with 100 as the *denominator* (the bottom line of a fraction).

  Example: $58.5\% = \dfrac{58.5}{100}$

- To change a fraction or decimal to a percentage, multiply by 100 and write the % sign next to the number.

  Example: find $\dfrac{6}{7} = \dfrac{6}{7} \times 100\%$

  $\dfrac{600}{7} = 85.75\%$

WORKED EXAMPLE 5.2

Find 40% of 3 kg.

Key question to ask yourself:

How do you find 1% of 3 kg?

Divide 3 kg by 100: $\dfrac{3\,\text{kg}}{100}$

Step 1: Find 1% of 3 kg

Step 2: Multiply by 40 to find 40% of 3 kg.

$$\frac{3\,\text{kg}}{100} \times 40 = 1.2\,\text{kg}$$

Questions

4 Complete this table. The first row has been done for you.

	Percentage	Decimal
5 m as a percentage of 20 m	$\dfrac{5}{20} \times 100 = 25\%$	0.25
10 minutes as a percentage of 50 minutes		
650 cm³ of a liquid as a percentage of 1250 cm³ of liquid		
55 g as a percentage of 800 g		

5 The total amount of input energy of a machine is 180 J. Find the percentage of energy wasted when the useful output energy is 45 J.

....

....

....

Maths focus 2: Calculating values using equations

Sometimes you need to adjust an equation to work out a value. This is called rearranging. You will find it easier to memorise equations if you learn just one version (see the Equations section at the back of the book). Then, if you know how to rearrange equations, you can get a different variable on its own on the left-hand side.

Here we will look at techniques for rearranging equations to get the value that you want. We will just look at equations that involve multiplication and division, because these are the ones you see most often in physics; for example, the link between mass and weight $W = mg$, the density equation $p = \dfrac{m}{v}$, the equation that defines resistance $R = \dfrac{V}{I}$.

What maths skills do you need to calculate values using equations?

1	Using two equations	• Choose the correct equations
		• Substitute known values
		• Swap the sides of an equation if necessary
		• Rearrange if necessary: multiply or divide by a value in order to isolate a variable
		• Use the 'found' value in the other equation
2	Using an equation of the form $\dfrac{y_1}{y_2} = \dfrac{x_1}{x_2}$	• Know that expressions that are ratios have no unit
		• Multiply and divide as necessary to isolate a variable
3	Understanding the effect of changing variable size	• Know the effect on answers of multiplying and dividing by larger and smaller numbers

Maths skills practice

How does rearranging an equation help us to find an unknown value?

When working out the value of an unknown variable from an equation, it is best if the unknown is on the left-hand side of the equals sign, because equations are read from left to right.

To do this you may need to rearrange an equation and make the unknown variable the subject.

As an example, resistance (R) is a measure of how hard it is for the potential difference (V) to make the current (I) flow. We use the equation

$$R = \frac{V}{I}$$

If you need to find the current, the equation needs rearranging to become

$$I = \frac{V}{R}$$

Once the current has been found, its value can be used to help find other values, such as the power wasted in the resistor using the equation

$$P = VI$$

Methods of rearranging equations are shown in Table 5.1. To rearrange equations easily, we should use some simple mathematical rules. Here are some examples.

- Any number or variable multiplied or divided by 1 stays the same, i.e. $\frac{b}{1} = b$.
- Any fraction showing a number or a variable divided by itself is equal to 1, i.e. $\frac{b}{b} = 1$

Therefore, a fraction such as $\frac{b}{b}$ can be cancelled and hence ignored in multiplication or division.

When rearranging an equation, we choose a value to multiply or divide by so that we can cancel. Read through Table 5.1, and look out for when this cancelling happens.

LOOK OUT

Remember that zx means $z \times x$.

Equation	What do you want to find? (the unknown variable)	How to do it	Example equation
$y = zx$	y	Multiply z by x	Finding weight from $W = mg$
$y = zx$	z (one of the two variables that are multiplied together)	Swap sides, then divide both sides by x: $z = \frac{y}{x}$	Finding mass from $W = mg$
$y = \frac{z}{x}$	y	Divide z by x	Finding pressure from $p = \frac{F}{A}$
$y = \frac{z}{x}$	z	Multiply both sides by x to get $yx = z$ Swap sides: $z = yx$	Finding a force from $p = \frac{F}{A}$
$y = \frac{z}{x}$	x	Multiply both sides by x to get $xy = z$ Then divide both sides by y: $x = \frac{z}{y}$	Finding area from $p = \frac{F}{A}$

Equation	What do you want to find? (the unknown variable)	How to do it	Example equation
$\dfrac{y_1}{y_2} = \dfrac{x_1}{x_2}$	y_1 (one of the variables on the top line)	Multiply both sides by the variable that y_1 is divided by, i.e $\dfrac{y_1 \, y_2}{y_2} = \dfrac{x_1 \, y_2}{x_2}$ Cancel: $y_1 = \dfrac{x_1 y_2}{x_2}$	Finding the number of turns on the primary coils of a transformer N_p from $\dfrac{N_p}{N_s} = \dfrac{V_p}{V_s}$
$\dfrac{y_1}{y_2} = \dfrac{x_1}{x_2}$	y_2 (one of the variables on the bottom line)	Multiply both sides by the unknown variable that you want to find, i.e. y_2. $\dfrac{y_1 y_2}{y_2} = \dfrac{x_1 y_2}{x_2}$ Cancel: $y_1 = \dfrac{x_1 y_2}{x_2}$ Then divide both sides by x_1 and multiply both sides by x_2. $\dfrac{y_1 x_2}{x_1} = y_2$ Swap sides: $y_2 = \dfrac{y_1 x_2}{x_1}$	Finding the number of turns on the primary coils of a transformer N_s from $\dfrac{N_p}{N_s} = \dfrac{V_p}{V_s}$

Table 5.1: Key methods of rearranging equations.

The pattern that you can see in Table 5.1 is:

- If the variable you want is at the top, divide both sides by any variable or number that is preventing the required variable being on its own.
- If the variable you want is at the bottom, multiply both sides by that variable to get it onto the top.

Maths skill 1: Using two equations

You have already seen how to substitute into equations where there is just one equation with one unknown. This section is about how the values found from one equation can be used in another equation. For instance, you can find out how much pressure a weight (weight is a force) exerts on an area from knowing its mass. This is by using $W = mg$ to find the weight, then using $p = \dfrac{F}{A}$, where the weight W is substituted as the force F.

WORKED EXAMPLE 5.3

Find the pressure, in N/m², exerted by a 500 g bag of sugar placed on a shelf. The surface area in contact with the shelf is 5 cm by 8 cm. The gravitational field strength is 9.8 N/kg.

Step 1: Check the units and ensure that they are consistent.

Convert each length into metres.

$5\,cm = 0.05\,m$

$8\,cm = 0.08\,m$

Step 2: Use the equation $W = mg$ to find the weight of the bag of sugar.

$W = 0.5\,kg \times 9.8\,N/kg$

$= 4.9\,N$

Step 3: Then using the equation for pressure, $p = \dfrac{F}{A}$, as weight is the force that acts on the surface, $F = W$. We can calculate the area of contact, A.

Area = length × width

$= 0.05\,m \times 0.08\,m$

$= 0.0040\,m^2$

Step 4: Substitute the values for force and area into the equation $p = \dfrac{F}{A}$.

$p\ (\text{in Pa}) = \dfrac{4.9\,N}{0.0040\,m^2}$

$= 1225\,Pa$

You can read more about the relationship between pressure, force and area in Chapter 5 of the Coursebook.

WORKED EXAMPLE 5.4

A boy lifts five boxes each of 150 N up a set of steps which are 4 m high. The average power he develops is 300 W. Which of the following is the time that he takes to run up the steps?

A 2 s   **B** 4 s   **C** 8 s   **D** 10 s

Step 1: List the values of the known variables and units. Check the units are consistent with each other.

$F = 150 \times 5 = 750\,N$

$d = 4\,m$

$t = ?\,s$

$P = 300\,W$

In this case the units are consistent.

1 watt = 1 joule per second   and   1 joule = 1 newton × 1 metre

There are no prefixes or inconsistent units to take into account.

CONTINUED

Step 2: Choose suitable equations and write them down. In this case,

energy transferred, $\Delta E = Fd$

and

power developed, $P = \dfrac{\Delta E}{t}$

These two equations link all of the information in the question.

Step 3: Firstly, choose the equation where there is only one unknown variable.

$\Delta E = Fd$

Substitute the values and find ΔE.

$\Delta E = 750\,\text{N} \times 4\,\text{m}$

$\Delta E = 3000\,\text{N}$

Step 4: You now have only one unknown in the second equation.

$P = \dfrac{\Delta E}{t}$

$300\,\text{W} = \dfrac{3000\,\text{N}}{t}$

Step 5: Rearrange to the equation to make time t the subject of the equation by multiplying both sides of the equation by t.

$300\,\text{W} \times t = 3000\,\text{N}$

Then divide both sides by $300\,\text{W}$.

$t = \dfrac{3000\,\text{N}}{300\,\text{W}}$

$t = 10\,\text{s}$

The answer is D.

Questions

6   A person of mass 55 kg gets into a raft. The sides of the raft are vertical. The surface area of the bottom of the boat in contact with water is 2.8 m². What is the increased pressure on the water when the person gets on board? The gravitational field strength is 9.8 N/kg.

Do you need to find the weight of the person before finding the change in pressure? Discuss with a friend.

....

....

....

7 **a** When the output potential difference from a power station is $30\,000\,\text{V}$, a current of $25\,000\,\text{A}$ flows. What is the output power in MW?

....

....

b Calculate the input power needed at the power station when the efficiency is 29%. Give your answer to 3 s.f.

....

....

8 The orbital period of the moon is 27.3 days. The average radius of the moon's orbit is $3.82 \times 10^8\,\text{m}$. Determine the average orbital speed of the moon.

....

....

....

Maths skill 2: Using an equation of the form $\dfrac{y_1}{y_2} = \dfrac{x_1}{x_2}$

When you use an equation of the form $\dfrac{y_1}{y_2} = \dfrac{x_1}{x_2}$, there will be three known values and one unknown.

$\dfrac{y_1}{y_2}$ is a **ratio**. A ratio is an expression which is a comparison of two numbers with the same unit. The ratio A to B can be written $A:B$, or expressed as a fraction $\dfrac{A}{B}$.

KEY WORD

ratio: a comparison of two numbers or two measurements with the same unit. The ratio A to B can be written $A:B$ or expressed as a fraction $\dfrac{A}{B}$

To calculate the value y_1, multiply both the left-hand side and the right-hand side by y_2. This isolates y_1.

The same method applies when calculating x_1. Multiply both the left-hand side and the right-hand side by x_2.

Worked example 5.5 asks you to find the variable x_2. You need to think carefully about this.

> **WORKED EXAMPLE 5.5**

A transformer has an input voltage of 120 V a.c. and output voltage of 10 V a.c. The number of turns on the primary coils is 1500. How many turns are on the secondary coil?

See Table 5.1 for more on methods of rearranging equations.

Step 1: List the known information from the question.

$$V_p = 120\,\text{V}$$
$$V_s = 10\,\text{V}$$
$$N_p = 1500$$
$$N_s = ?$$

Step 2: Choose the equation that gives only one unknown.

$$\frac{V_p}{V_s} = \frac{N_p}{N_s}$$

Step 3: Substitute the values into the equation.

$$\frac{120\,\text{V}}{10\,\text{V}} = \frac{1500}{N_s}$$

Step 4: Multiply both sides by N_s to make N_s appear on the top line.

$$N_s \times \frac{120\,\text{V}}{10\,\text{V}} = 1500$$

Step 5: Isolate N_s by multiplying both sides of the equation by 10 and then dividing both sides by 120.

$$N_s \times \frac{120\,\text{V}}{10\,\text{V}} \times 10 = 1500 \times 10$$
$$N_s \times 120 \div 120 = 15\,000 \div 120$$
$$N_s = 125$$

Alternatively, simplify the fraction on the left-hand side of the equation:

Step 5: Simplify the fraction on the left-hand side of the equation.

$$N_s \times 12 = 1500$$

Step 6: Divide both sides by 12 to isolate N_s.

$$N_s = 125$$

You can read more about transformers in Chapter 21 of the Coursebook.

Questions

9   A transformer is used to change a voltage of 25 000 V to 140 000 V. It has 5000 turns on its primary coil. How many turns does it have on its secondary coil?

....

....

10 To find out if a crystal is a diamond, an optical experiment is done to compare its refractive index with that of diamond. Measurements of the angle of incidence, i, and the angle of refraction, r, are taken, and then compared to similar measurements for a diamond.

	Diamond	Crystal
i / °	20.0	10.0
r / °	8.2	A

Table 5.2: Angles of incidence and refraction for diamond and unknown cystal.

What value would you expect to find for angle of refraction A in Table 5.2, if the crystal is a real diamond? Show your working and give your answer to 2 s.f.

....

....

....

....

Maths skill 3: Understanding the effect of changing variable size

KEY WORD

product: the result of multiplying two or more values

Changing the size of the values in an equation can have a significant effect on the outcome.

If two numbers are multiplied together, for example, $a \times b$:

- when one of the numbers a or b gets bigger, the **product** becomes bigger

- when one of the numbers is less than 1, the product is smaller than the other number. For example, if $a = 14$ and $b = 0.5$, then the product is $14 \times 0.5 = 7.0$.

If one number is divided by another, for example, $\frac{a}{b}$:

- when a gets bigger, the answer becomes bigger

- when b gets bigger, the answer becomes smaller (see Worked example 5.6).

WORKED EXAMPLE 5.6

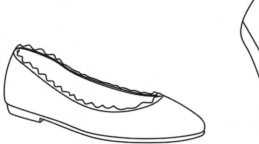

Figure 5.1: Shoes with different heel areas exert different pressures.

A woman who weighs 450 N wears a pair of flat shoes (Figure 5.1). Each shoe has a surface area of 250 cm² in contact with the ground.

a   What pressure does she exert on the ground?

b   She then changes into stiletto shoes that each have a contact surface area of 75 cm².

What is the new pressure?

a   **Step 1:**   Choose the pressure equation.

$$\text{Pressure} = \frac{\text{force}}{\text{area}}$$

   Step 2:   Substitute the values for the first set of shoes. Don't forget the area needs be multiplied by two as people wear a *pair* of shoes.

$$\text{Pressure} = \frac{450\,\text{N}}{2 \times 250\,\text{cm}^2}$$
$$= 0.9\,\text{N/cm}^2$$

b   **Step 1:**   The woman has changed the shoes to stilettos, with a narrow heel. Substitute the values for the stilettos.

$$\text{Pressure} = \frac{450\,\text{N}}{2 \times 75\,\text{cm}^2}$$
$$= 3\,\text{N/cm}^2$$

The reduction in the surface area has caused an increase in the pressure.

Practical Investigation 5.3 in the Practical Workbook investigates the relationship between the surface area of shoes and pressure on the ground.

WORKED EXAMPLE 5.7

A machine transfers 6000 J of energy in 0.2 s. What is the effect of transferring the same amount of energy in 10 s?

Step 1: Choose the equation that links the variables with only one unknown.

$$\text{Power} = \frac{\text{change in energy}}{\text{time}}$$

$$= \frac{\Delta E}{t}$$

Step 2: Substitute the data into the equation.

$$\text{Power} = \frac{6000\,\text{J}}{0.2\,\text{s}}$$

$$= 30\,000\,\text{W}$$

This shows that 30 000 J of energy is being transferred every second.

Step 3: Repeat the substitution with the larger value for time.

$$\text{Power} = \frac{6000\,\text{J}}{10\,\text{s}}$$

$$= 600\,\text{W}$$

By lengthening the time for the transfer, the power is reduced. The rate of energy transfer is reduced.

Questions

11 An astronaut has a mass of 90 kg.

a Calculate the weight of the astronaut on the Earth, where the gravitational field strength is 9.8 N/kg.

....

b Calculate the weight of the astronaut on Pluto, where the gravitational field strength is 0.6 N/kg.

....

c The weight of the same astronaut on a new planet is 1450 N. What is the gravitational field strength on the new planet? Give your answer to 2 s.f.

....

12 A student is told that the smaller the current caused by a potential difference is, the greater is the circuit resistance.

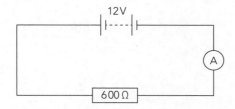

Figure 5.2: Circuit to measure the current.

When the student changes the resistor in the circuit in Figure 5.2, the current changes from 0.02 A to 0.6 mA. What is the value of the new resistance? Was the information given to the student correct?

....

....

....

....

Maths focus 3: Doing more complex calculations

Many problems in physics are complex and may need more than two equations to solve them. You need to consider how the result of one equation can be used in another. It is helpful to know that the same variable may be in several equations. Energy is a good example (see the spider diagram in Figure 5.3).

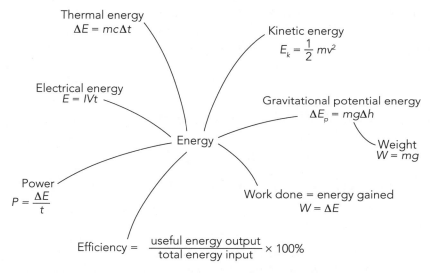

Figure 5.3: The quantity 'energy', symbol E, appears in many equations in physics.

With a common variable, equations can be linked together. For example, the work done in lifting an object equals the gravitational potential energy gained by the object. If the time taken for the lifting is known, the power can be calculated. Which equations in Figure 5.3 would be used?

What maths skills do you need to do more complex calculations?

1	Doing calculations involving several equations	• Record the information that you know and what you need to find
		• Choose the correct equations to work with
		• Work out the sequence in which to apply equations
		• Apply BIDMAS
2	Adding reciprocals	• Add fractions
		• Find unknown variables

Maths skills practice

How do complex calculations help with problem-solving in physics?

You might need to calculate the efficiency and the power of someone going upstairs, when you are only given the person's weight, change in height and the time taken. This would need several calculations using equations involving energy.   .

Maths skill 1: Doing calculations involving several equations

As with all problems, you need to start by writing down the values of the variables you know and list the variable you are trying to find. From this, you can start with an equation with one unknown. The information gained from this answer can then be used in another equation.

When you *read* an equation, you read from left to right, just like reading sentences in English. But, when working out the mathematics in an equation such as the equation for gravitational potential energy, $\Delta E_p = mg\Delta h$, which can be written $\Delta E_p = mg(h_2 - h_1)$, the *order of calculation* is not always left to right.   .

> **LOOK OUT**
>
> Go through the Equations section at the back of this book. Look out for variables that re-occur.

> **LOOK OUT**
>
> The symbol Δ means 'change in'.

> **KEY WORD**
>
> **BIDMAS:** 'Brackets, Indices, Division/Multiplication, Addition/Subtraction', which is the order in which mathematical operations are done in a multi-step calculation

It is helpful to remember the term **BIDMAS**, which reminds you about which parts of a calculation to do first:

Brackets, **I**ndices (powers), **D**ivision, **M**ultiplication, **A**ddition, **S**ubtraction

WORKED EXAMPLE 5.8

A machine uses 500 J of energy to lift a 20 N object from a platform that is 4 m high to a roof that is 18 m high. It develops a useful power of 600 W. Calculate the input power.

Key question to ask yourself:

- Which equations do you know, relevant to this context, that contain these variables?

  Gravitational potential energy $= \Delta E_p = mg\Delta h$

  $$\text{Efficiency} = \frac{\text{useful energy output}}{\text{total energy input}} \times 100\%$$

  $$\text{Efficiency} = \frac{\text{useful power output}}{\text{total power input}} \times 100\%$$

- Which of these equations has only one unknown value?

We have all the information to calculate the gravitational potential energy, $\Delta E_p = mg\Delta h$.

Step 1: List the values of the known variables and units.

   Input energy = 500 J
   Force = 20 N
   Starting height = 4 m
   Finishing height = 18 m
   Input power = ?
   Output power = 600 W

Step 2: The equation $\Delta E_p = mg\Delta h$ includes the change in height, Δh, so you need to work this out first. This is the same as working out the brackets in BIDMAS, since the equation can be written as $\Delta E_p = mg(h_2 - h_1)$. The change in height Δh is $h_2 - h_1$.

   Change in height, $\Delta h = 18\,\text{m} - 4\,\text{m}$
   $= 14\,\text{m}$

Step 3: Then $\Delta E_p = mg\Delta h$
   $= 20\,\text{N} \times 14\,\text{m}$
   $= 280\,\text{J}$

Step 4: Link ΔE_p to the useful energy transferred.

   Energy transferred (output energy) $= \Delta E_p$
   $= 280\,\text{J}$

CONTINUED

Step 5:   Link input energy, useful energy transferred (output) and efficiency together. There are two knowns and one unknown.

$$\text{Efficiency} = \frac{\text{useful energy output}}{\text{total energy input}} \times 100\%$$

$$= \frac{280\,\text{J}}{500\,\text{J}} \times 100\%$$

$$= 56\%$$

Step 6:   We need to find the input power. Link this with the efficiency equation expressed in terms of power.

$$\text{Efficiency} = \frac{\text{useful power output}}{\text{total power input}} \times 100\%$$

$$So,\quad 56\% = \frac{600\,\text{W}}{\text{total power output}} \times 100\%$$

Step 7:   Rearrange the equation to give *total* power input.

$$\textit{Total}\ \text{power input} = \frac{600\,\text{W}}{56} \times 100$$

$$= 1100\,\text{W to 2 s.f.}$$

Questions

13 Make a spider diagram, similar to that in Figure 5.3, for either mass or force.

14 The power used by a 1.5 V calculator is $5.0 \times 10^{-5}\,\text{W}$. When the '=' button is pressed, the current flows for $1.6 \times 10^{-7}\,\text{s}$.

  a   Calculate the current from the battery.

  ....

  ....

LOOK OUT

It is important not to round values to two significant figures prematurely at intermediate stages within a calculation, because this may lead to an incorrect final answer. You should wait until you obtain a final answer before rounding to an appropriate number of significant figures.

b What is the resistance of the circuits in the calculator?

....

....

c How much energy is transferred in the process?

....

....

Maths skill 2: Adding reciprocals

In the design of electric circuits, it is essential to be able to work out the resistance, current and voltages of components in different circuits.

If resistors are in parallel, as in Figure 5.4, the potential difference V across each one is the same. The total current shown by the symbol I_T equals the *sum* of the current in each of the branches of the circuit.

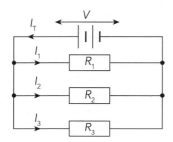

Figure 5.4: Resistors in parallel.

$$I_T = I_1 + I_2 + I_3$$

Also $\quad I_1 = \dfrac{V}{R_1}, I_2 = \dfrac{V}{R_2}, I_3 = \dfrac{V}{R_3} \quad$ and $\quad I_T = \dfrac{V}{R_T}$

where R_T is the total (effective) resistance of the parallel resistors.

Therefore

$$\frac{V}{R_T} = \frac{V}{R_1} + \frac{V}{R_2} + \frac{V}{R_s}$$

Dividing both sides of the equation by V gives

$$\frac{1}{R_T} = \frac{1}{R_1} + \frac{1}{R_2} + \frac{1}{R_s}$$

This allows you to calculate R_T.

WORKED EXAMPLE 5.9

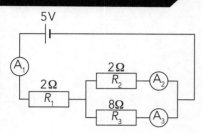

Figure 5.5: Circuit to measure the current through resistors in parallel and series.

A 5 V cell allows a current to flow in the circuit shown in Figure 5.5. Find the total resistance of the resistors in parallel, and the total resistance in the circuit.

Key question to ask yourself:

- Which combination of resistors is in parallel?

  R_2 and R_3 are in parallel.

- How can the total resistance of this parallel section of the circuit be labelled?

  R_p is appropriate.

- Which combination of resistors is in series?

  R_1 and R_p are in series.

Step 1: Write down the equation involving R_p.

$$\frac{1}{R_p} = \frac{1}{R_2} + \frac{1}{R_3}$$

$$\frac{1}{R_p} = \frac{1}{2} + \frac{1}{8}$$

Using fraction arithmetic:

$$\frac{1}{R_p} = \frac{4+1}{8}$$

$$\frac{1}{R_p} = \frac{5}{8}$$

$$R_p = 1.6\,\Omega$$

Step 2: As R_p and R_1 are in series, they can be added to find R_T, the total resistance.

$$R_T = 1.6\,\Omega + 2\,\Omega$$

$$= 3.6\,\Omega$$

Questions

15 Calculate the total resistance in the circuit shown in Figure 5.6.

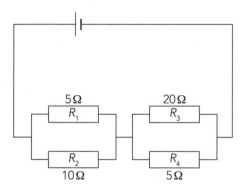

Figure 5.6: Two pairs of resistors in parallel.

....

....

....

16 What is the resistance of component R_B when a potential difference of 36 V causes a total current of 4 mA to flow in the circuit in Figure 5.7? Circle A, B, C or D. Explain your answer.

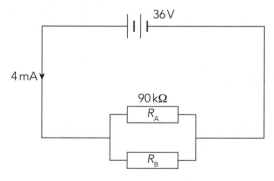

Figure 5.7: Circuit to find an unknown resistance in parallel.

A 9 mΩ   **B** 10 mΩ   **C** 9 kΩ   **D** 10 kΩ

....

....

....

....

Maths focus 4: Calculations that involve direction: moments and momentum

The direction in which a force acts is important to the outcome. When a force is causing an object to turn, for example, when a weight is put on one end of a beam, the size of the force and the direction of turning should be taken into account in any calculations.

What maths skills do you need in calculations that involve direction?

1	Calculating moments	•	Recognise clockwise ↻ and anticlockwise ↺ directions
		•	Apply the principle of moments: ↺ moment = ↻ moment for objects in equilibrium (balanced)
		•	Apply the rule: upwards force is equal and opposite to downwards force for objects in equilibrium
2	Solving momentum problems	•	Apply direction to momentum calculations
		•	Choose and apply the correct momentum equation

Maths skills practice

How is direction important in physics problems?

In many situations, the direction of a force or the direction of motion is important to the outcome. Here are just two examples:

* If you are pushing on a door to open it and someone else also pushes it, the *direction* of the push from the other person can make it harder or easier for you to open the door.

* When you are driving a bumper car and are hit by another one, the *direction* in which you are each initially moving affects the impact.

Maths skill 1: Calculating moments

The *moment* of a force is a measure of the turning effect of a force. The direction of the force is important (Figure 5.8).

When an object is balanced (not turning):

- sum of the anticlockwise moments = sum of the clockwise moments (the principle of moments)

Also, as in any physics problem involving equilibrium:

- sum of the upwards forces = sum of the downwards forces.

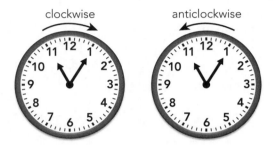

Figure 5.8: Clockwise and anticlockwise directions.

WORKED EXAMPLE 5.10

Three children are playing on a see-saw that is pivoted in the middle. Where must Arun sit if the see-saw is to be balanced (i.e. in equilibrium)?

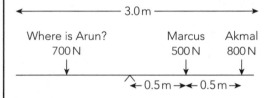

Figure 5.9: See-saw.

Key question to ask yourself:

Which forces are tending to turn the see-saw anticlockwise about the pivot, and which are tending to turn it clockwise?

Arun's weight causes an anticlockwise moment, while Marcus and Akmal contribute to a clockwise moment.

Step 1:   Work out the total of the anticlockwise moments caused by Arun.

$$\text{Anticlockwise moment} = \text{force} \times \text{perpendicular distance from the pivot}$$
$$= 700\,\text{N} \times d\,\text{m}$$

Don't worry that this equation includes an unknown variable. It is the one we want to find: d is what we are calling the distance from the pivot to where Arun sits.

CONTINUED

Step 2:   Work out the total of the clockwise moments caused by Marcus and Akmal.

Marcus's clockwise moment = force × perpendicular distance from the pivot

$$= 500\,\text{N} \times 0.5\,\text{m}$$

$$= 250\,\text{Nm}$$

Akmal's clockwise moment = force × perpendicular distance from the pivot

$$= 800\,\text{N} \times 1.0\,\text{m}$$

$$= 800\,\text{Nm}$$

Total clockwise moment $= 250\,\text{Nm} + 800\,\text{Nm}$

$$= 1050\,\text{Nm}$$

Step 3:   Apply the principle of moments.

Total anticlockwise moments = total clockwise moments

$$700d = 1050$$

Step 4:   Isolate d by dividing both sides of the equation by 700.

$$d = \frac{1050}{700}$$

$$= 1.5\,\text{m}$$

Therefore, Arun should sit 1.5 m from the pivot.

You can read more about the moment of a force in Chapter 4 in the Coursebook.

Question

17 A crane, used to lift heavy steel girders, has a jib (arm) 30 m long. There is a concrete balancing weight of 10 000 N positioned at one end of the jib, 5 m from the pivot as shown in Figure 5.10. What is the maximum weight of girders the crane can lift? Assume the jib has no mass.

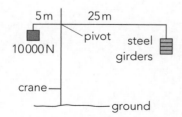

Figure 5.10: A crane lifting steel girders.

....

....

Maths skill 2: Solving momentum problems

Momentum is defined as the product of the mass and the velocity of a moving object, that is mass multiplied by velocity. It is a **vector** quantity, which means its value includes its direction. Its direction will be that of the velocity.

See Chapter 6 for more on vectors.

We only need to consider motion in a straight line. Velocity and momentum values in one direction are positive, and in the opposite direction they are negative.

There are three main equations in which momentum features:

1   momentum = mass × velocity

       $p = mv$

2   momentum before an event = momentum after the event

      This is called the *conservation of momentum*.

      For two objects, 1 and 2, involved in a collision (Figure 5.11)

        $m_1u_1 + m_2u_2 = m_1v_1 + m_2v_2$

      where u_1 and u_2 represent the velocity of objects 1 and 2 before the collision, and v_1 and v_2 represent the velocity of each after the collision.

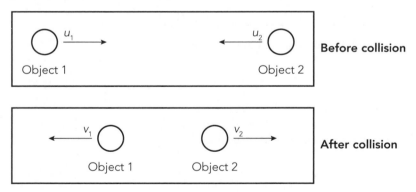

Figure 5.11: The conservation of momentum for two objects.

3   impulse on an object = force × change in time

$Ft = mv - mu$

force × time = mass × final velocity – mass × initial velocity

You can think about impulse in two different ways:

- the force on the object multiplied by the period of time over which it acts
- the change in momentum of the object.

Practical investigation 3.3 in the Practical Workbook investigates momentum between two trolleys involved in an explosion situation.

WORKED EXAMPLE 5.11

A person jumps from a small stationary boat onto the shore, with a velocity of 2 m/s. The boat moves away from the shore, as shown in Figure 5.12. What is the velocity of the boat as the person leaves it?

The person's mass is 75 kg and the boat's mass is 200 kg.

Figure 5.12: As the person jumps out of the boat, the boat moves away from the shore.

Key question to ask yourself:

Which of the momentum equations are relevant?

The conservation of momentum equation is the relevant one here:

$$m_1 u_1 + m_2 u_2 = m_1 v_1 + m_2 v_2$$

Step 1:   Apply the conservation of momentum.

Before the jump, the combined momentum $m_1 u_1 + m_2 u_2$ of the person and the boat was zero. Therefore, the total momentum $m_1 v_1 + m_2 v_2$ after the jump must be zero:

$$0 = m_1 v_1 + m_2 v_2$$

where m_1 is the mass of the person, m_2 is the mass of the boat, v_1 is the velocity of the person and v_2 is the velocity of the boat.

CONTINUED

Step 2: Rearrange the equation.

$$v_2 = -\frac{m_1 v_1}{m_2}$$

The minus sign means that the boat is moving in the opposite direction to the person.

Step 3: Substitute values.

$$v_2 = -\frac{m_1 v_1}{m_2}$$

$$v_2 = -\frac{75 \times 2}{200}$$

$$v_2 = -0.75 \, \text{m/s}$$

$$= -1 \, \text{m/s rounded to the 2 s.f. of the data in the question}$$

Questions

18 Two objects with masses of 10 kg and 11 kg move towards each other with velocities of 20 m/s and 5 m/s respectively. They join together and move as one body.

    a What is the common speed of the objects just after the collision? Give your answer to 2 s.f.

    ....

    ....

    b In which direction do they move?

    ....

19 A person releases the air, of mass 1.8 g, from an inflated balloon, as in Figure 5.13. The air escapes from the balloon at 2.0 m/s. The balloon deflates at a steady rate for 4.0 s. What is the forward impulsive force exerted on the neck of the balloon?

2.0

Figure 5.13: Air escaping from a balloon.

....

....

....

20 The producers of a film want to make two identical bullets have a head-on collision and melt. They need to ensure that the kinetic energy of the bullets is sufficient to melt the metal (lead) when they collide.

The melting point of lead is 327 °C. The specific heat capacity of lead is 130 J/kg °C.

The temperature of the bullets before impact is 23 °C.

What speed will the bullets need to reach?

Assume that all of the kinetic energy is transferred to thermal energy.
Give your answer to 3 s.f.

....

....

....

....

21 A mass of 20 kg has a constant force acting on it for 5 s. This produces an increase in momentum of 30 Ns. When the same force acts for 35 s on a mass of 10 kg, what is the increase in momentum of this mass?

....

....

Maths focus 5: Radioactive decay calculations

In mathematics, you cannot add two different things together and come out with a total, unless you carefully define what you are adding. You need to be really careful with the wording you use. For example, adding 6 protons to 11 neutrons and coming out with 17 as an answer does not make sense. Are the 17 protons or neutrons?

However, if you add 6 'particles with mass' (nucleons) in the nucleus to 11 other 'particles with mass' (nucleons) in the same nucleus then the *total number of particles with mass* (nucleons) is 17. The *wording* really matters.

What maths skills do you need when you do radioactive decay calculations?

1	Doing particle calculations	• Know when particles can be added together
		• Balance radioactive decay equations
2	Interpreting half-life informataion	• Choose correctly between halving values or doubling values as time goes forwards or backwards
		• Count the number of half-lives elapsed

Maths skills practice

How does knowing the decay pattern and the half-life of a radioactive material affect choices?

Applications of radioactive decay are an important part of the modern world. As a society, we need to understand the processes involved, so that safe decisions can be taken. In medicine, radioactive materials can be low-risk if used appropriately. Radioactive tracers, for example, which are used in diagnosis, need to have short half-lives, emissions that will cause minimum harm, and decay products that are safe inside the human body.

You can read more about radioactive decay in Chapter 23 of the Coursebook.

Maths skill 1: Doing particle calculations

Radioactive decay can be represented by equations that use special notation. For example:

$$^{241}_{95}\text{Am} \rightarrow {}^{237}_{92}\text{Np} + {}^{4}_{2}\text{He}$$

- The chemical symbol represents the nucleus of a particular element.

- The number at the top left of the chemical symbol represents the total mass of the nucleus. It is the total number of nucleons (protons plus neutrons).

- The number at the bottom left of the chemical symbol is the number of protons in the nucleus. See Figure 5.14.

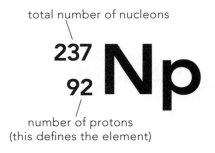

total number of nucleons

$$^{237}_{92}\text{Np}$$

number of protons
(this defines the element)

Figure 5.14: Nuclide notation used in decay equations.

If the element produced in a decay is unknown, X is used for the chemical symbol. The proton number defines the element.

The symbols we use for alpha and beta particles in decay equations are shown in Table 5.3.

Particle	Symbol
alpha	$^{4}_{2}\text{He}$
beta	$^{0}_{-1}\text{e}$

Table 5.3: Symbols used for alpha and beta particles in decay equations.

The lower number -1 for the beta particle refers to its charge: one proton has charge $+1$ and one electron has charge -1.

LOOK OUT

Radioactive decay equations have an arrow, not an equals sign. The arrow is read aloud as becomes.

LOOK OUT

An electron is not a nucleon, so its nucleon number is zero. You cannot add electrons and nucleons. Only the charges can be added.

WORKED EXAMPLE 5.12

When thorium $^{232}_{90}$Th decays, an alpha particle is emitted. Write the equation which describes this process.

Step 1: Identify the particle that is emitted and its associated symbol. It is an alpha (α) particle, which is $^4_2$He.

Step 2: Decide whether the information given relates to the element that decays, or to the element that is produced.

Thorium is the starting element that decays.

Step 3: Write the equation using X as the unknown element.

Work out the number of nucleons (upper number) of the new element X, and then the number of protons (lower number).

Do this by ensuring the numbers are the same on both sides.

Nucleons: $232 \rightarrow \mathbf{228} + 4$

Protons: $90 \rightarrow \mathbf{88} + 2$

$^{232}_{90}\text{Th} \rightarrow {}^{228}_{88}\text{X} + {}^4_2\text{He}$

Step 4: Consult the Periodic Table to find the chemical symbol of the element with this number of protons. Replace the X with its chemical symbol. The element with an atomic number of 88 is radium, symbol Ra.

$^{232}_{90}\text{Th} \rightarrow {}^{228}_{88}\text{Ra} + {}^4_2\text{H}$

Questions

22 The nucleus of the radioactive isotope of radon, $^{222}_{86}$Rn, emits an alpha particle. Write down the equation that represents this event.

....

23 When carbon $^{14}_6$C decays, a β-particle is emitted. Work out the equation that represents this process.

....

24 These symbols represent different radioactive nuclides.

$^{98}_{52}\text{P}$ $^{99}_{52}\text{Q}$ $^{94}_{50}\text{S}$ $^{99}_{51}\text{T}$

a Which nuclide has the smallest mass? ....

b Which nuclide has the largest number of neutrons? ....

c Write an equation using two of these nuclides, where one decays to the other by alpha emission.

....

d Write an equation using two of these nuclides, where one decays to the other by beta emission.

....

Maths skill 2: Interpreting half-life information

The half-life of a radioactive element is the average length of time it takes for half of the nuclei in a sample to decay.

It is also the length of time it takes for the activity (number of decays per second) to fall to half.

WORKED EXAMPLE 5.13

The half-life of francium-223 is 22 minutes. Complete the missing figures in the table.

Time / minutes	Count rate / counts/s
0	800
22	
	200
66	100
110	25

Step 1: In the first column, look for the pattern showing how time increases.

The time increases by 22 minutes for each reading.

Therefore, the pattern should be: 0, 22, 44, 66, 88, 110.

Step 2: Knowing that the count rate decreases by half every 22 minutes (because this is the half-life), work out each missing count rate value from its preceding one.

At 22 minutes, the count rate will be half the value of the count rate at the beginning:

$$\frac{800}{2} = 400 \, \text{counts/s}$$

At 88 minutes, the count rate will be half the value of the count rate at the beginning:

$$\frac{100}{2} = 50 \, \text{counts/s}$$

CONTINUED

The final table should read as shown in Table 5.4.

Time / minutes	Count rate counts / s
0	800
22	**400**
44	200
66	100
88	**50**
110	25

Table 5.4: Completed half-life table for Worked example 5.13.

Practical Investigation 23.1 in the Practical Workbook investigates radioactive decay and the half-life of isotopes using a model.

WORKED EXAMPLE 5.14

Carbon $^{14}_{6}C$ has a half-life of 5730 years. The $^{14}_{6}C$ is produced in the upper atmosphere and becomes part of the carbon cycle: when living organisms interact with the atmosphere they absorb $^{14}_{6}C$. The proportion of $^{14}_{6}C$ in living organisms is constant. When the organism dies, no more $^{14}_{6}C$ is absorbed and the known amount of $^{14}_{6}C$ begins to decay. When a tree died it had 200 units of $^{14}_{6}C$ and as a fossil it has 25 units. How old is the fossil? Give your answer to 3 s.f.

Key question to ask yourself:

Which is the better choice: to work from the most recent value and work backwards in time, or to work forwards in time?

In this case there is enough information to work either way.

Step 1: Look for the information given: the known amount of material or known count rate.

In this case we know the starting amount and the final amount of $^{14}_{6}C$: 200 units and 25 units.

Step 2: Decide whether to count forwards or backwards in time.

We will count forwards from the start.

Step 3: Work out the number of units of $^{14}_{6}C$ after each half-life, by repeatedly halving the amount of material, until the final, known value is reached.

200   100   50   25
    5730 y   5730 y   5730 y

Step 4: Add up the number of years:

3×5730 years = 17 190 years

The fossil is 17 200 years old, to 3 s.f.

Questions

25 Radioactive iodine, which has a half-life of 8 days, is used in hospitals to treat people with tumours in the thyroid gland. The initial count rate is 3.0×10^6 counts/s. Which answer shows the activity after 16 days? Circle A, B, C or D.

A 1.25×10^6 counts/s   **B** 0.75×10^6 counts/s

C 1.5×10^6 counts/s   **D** 5.0×10^3 counts/s

26 An isotope, dysprosium-165, is used as an aggregated hydroxide for treatment of arthritis. Its half-life is 2 hours. At 7.00 p.m., the activity of a sample of dysprosium-165 is 10 counts/s. Calculate the activity at 7.00 a.m. that morning.

....

....

27 An isotope of a radioactive material has a half-life of 7.5 hours. After what period of time is the amount of radioactive material reduced by 75% of its initial value? Circle A, B, C or D.

A $\frac{3}{4}$ hours   **B** $\frac{1}{4}$ hours   **D** 22.5 hours   **C** 15 hours

---

EXAM-STYLE QUESTIONS

1 A student makes a working model of the water-powered turbine. In this model, falling water is used to turn turbines which are connected to generators to produce electricity.

Every second 100 g of water falls on the turbines from the height of 10 cm.

a Calculate the weight of 100 g of water in newtons. (Take $g = 9.8$ N/kg)

....

....

Weight = ... N   **[2]**

b Determine the energy transferred in 1 second by the falling water to the turbine.

....

....

....

....

Energy transferred in 1 second = ... unit ....   **[4]**

CONTINUED

c   The power output of the generator is 5 mW. Find the efficiency of the model prepared by the student.

....

....

Efficiency = ...   [2]

[Total: 8]

2   A bag of mass 2 kg is lifted to the height of 12 m. (Take g = 9.8 N/kg)

a   Determine the weight of the bag.

....

....

Weight = ... unit ....   [2]

b   Calculate the work done on the bag to take it 12 m high.

....

....

Work done = ... unit ....   [2]

c   Find the change in the gravitational potential energy of the bag.

....

Change in gravitational potential energy = ... unit .... [1]

[Total: 5]

3   A current of 10 A flows through a resistor when the potential difference across the resistor is 12 V.

a   Calculate the power used in the resistor.

Power = ... unit ....   [2]

b   Calculate the electric charge flowing through the resistor in 1 second.

Charge = ... unit ....   [2]

[Total: 4]

4 A 120 cm fluorescent light fitting is suspended from a ceiling by two chains that produce forces F_1 and F_2 as in Figure 5.15.

F_1 acts 10 cm from one end. F_2 acts 15 cm from the other end. The weight of the light is 15 N. The pivot is marked as A.

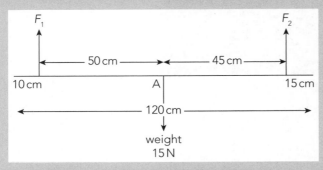

Figure 5.15: Forces diagram for a light fitting.

a State an expression relating F_1 and F_2. [1]

....

b Give expressions for clockwise and anticlockwise moments about point A.

i Clockwise moment = ...

ii Anticlockwise moment = ... [2]

c Calculate the tension forces F_1 and F_2 in the chains.

....

....

....

F_1 = ... F_2 = ... [3]

[Total: 6]

CONTINUED

5   The Black eye galaxy is 17 million light-years away from Earth.
    (1 light-year = 9.5×10^{15} m)

    a   Calculate the distance of the Black Eye galaxy in kilometres
        from Earth.

        ....

        ....

    Distance = ... km   [1]

    b   A new galaxy has been observed to be moving away from Earth at
        speed of 408 km/s. Calculate the distance between Earth and
        the galaxy.

        Give your answer to 2 s.f. (2.2×10^{-18}/s)

        ....

        ....

        ....

    Distance = ... km   [3]

                                                               [Total: 4]

Working with shape

Maths focus 1: Solving problems involving shape

When you are reading a physics text that involves the shape of an object, a diagram can help you to understand the description. A diagram can give you information that would take many sentences to describe. However, you need to be able to interpret the diagram.

What maths skills do you need to solve problems involving shape?

1	Extracting information from diagrams	•	Interpret diagrams
		•	Recognise common shapes and know important terms relating to shape
2	Calculating using the mathematics of shape	•	Recall the equations relating to shape
		•	Calculate lengths, areas and volumes of different shapes
		•	Apply the shape equations to real situations

Maths skills practice

How does understanding shape help with physics problems?

In physics, the shape and dimensions of objects often affect the values of variables. If a gas is squashed into a smaller volume (while its temperature is kept constant), its pressure increases. If a force is exerted over a smaller area, the pressure on the surface increases.

KEY WORD

surface area: the total area of the surface of a three-dimensional object

A hot material cools faster when its **surface area** is large, because thermal energy is lost from the surface of an object. Evaporation is more effective when the surface area of the wet material is made larger. Laundry dries more quickly when it is hung on a washing line than it would sitting in a washing basket.

Sometimes we need to use equations that involve shape variables, for example:

$$\text{density} = \frac{\text{mass}}{\text{volume}} \quad \text{and} \quad \text{pressure} = \frac{\text{force}}{\text{area}}$$

Maths skill 1: Extracting information from diagrams

Diagrams show how objects are arranged. For example, they can show us which volume or surface area is being referred to. You need to think about how you view diagrams so that you can correctly interpret what they show.

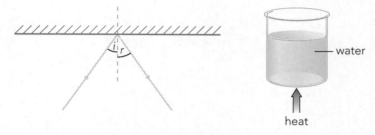

Figure 6.1: Two examples of diagrams.

There are three main categories of diagrams:

- diagrams that use an agreed set of symbols to show apparatus, for example electric circuit diagrams and ray diagrams (Figure 6.1)

- diagrams that are a very simplified picture of apparatus or of a situation

- diagrams that are a combination of the above two types; for example, diagrams showing the forces acting on an object (Figure 6.2).

Figure 6.2: Diagram showing the forces acting on an object.

When looking at diagrams, first consider:

- Is the diagram showing you a static situation (Figure 6.3)?

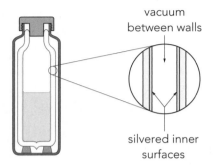

vacuum
between walls

silvered inner
surfaces

Figure 6.3: Diagram of a vacuum flask: a static situation.

- Is the diagram showing a process (Figure 6.4)?

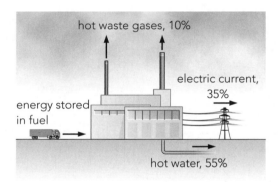

hot waste gases, 10%

electric current, 35%

energy stored in fuel

hot water, 55%

Figure 6.4: Diagram of the processes in a power station.

Then consider:

- Is the diagram showing two dimensions (2D) or three dimensions (3D) (Figure 6.5)?

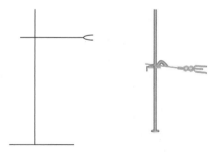

Figure 6.5: Two-dimensional and three-dimensional diagrams of the same object.

Finally, consider:

- Is the diagram an overhead view (a 'plan'), or a sideways view?

You need to be sure that you know the meanings of key mathematical words used when describing diagrams. Some important ones are shown in Figure 6.6.

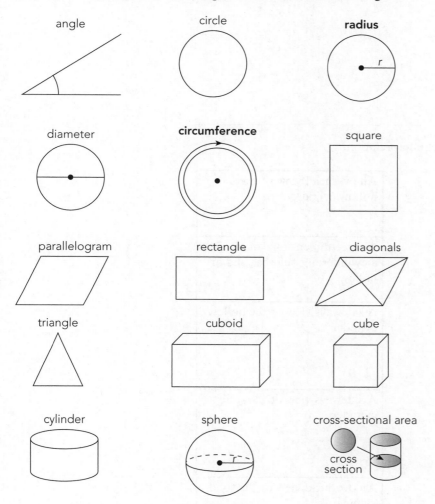

Figure 6.6: Key words relating to diagrams.

KEY WORDS

circumference: the distance around a circle

radius: the result of multiplying two or more values

WORKED EXAMPLE 6.1 ▶

The diagrams A to E in Table 6.1 are all different views of one of the two cylinders shown in Figure 6.7.

solid cylinder   hollow cylinder

Figure 6.7: Two cylinders.

Link each of diagrams A to E to its correct interpretation.

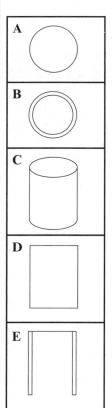

A ○	An overhead view of the hollow cylinder
B ◎	A three-dimensional view of a cylinder; it could be solid or hollow
C (cylinder)	A sideways view of the hollow cylinder
D □	A sideways view of the solid cylinder
E ⊓	An overhead view of the solid cylinder

Table 6.1: Link each diagram to the correct definition.

Step 1: Check whether the text gives you information.

The diagrams are described as either *hollow* or *solid* cylinders.

Step 2: Is the view three-dimensional?

C is the only three-dimensional one.

CONTINUED

Step 3: Is the view from overhead or sideways?

A and B are overhead views, D and E are sideways views.

Step 4: Is the view showing a hollow cylinder or a solid one? A and D are solid, B and E are hollow

Step 5: Using the information obtained, sort out which picture matches each description.

A is an overhead view of the solid cylinder.

B is an overhead view of the hollow cylinder.

D is a sideways view of the solid cylinder.

E is a sideways view of the hollow cylinder.

Questions

1 Which of the definitions in Table 6.2 describes a shape? Circle A, B, C or D

A	radius	The distance across a circle.
B	circumference	The distance around a circle.
C	cuboid	A three dimensional block with six identical square faces.
D	diagonal	The line that goes from one side of a circle to the other by going through the centre.

Table 6.2: Which of these is a shape?

2

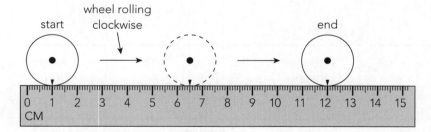

Figure 6.8: Toy wheel rolling along a ruler.

A small toy wheel is rolled along a horizontal ruler (Figure 6.8). The wheel is rolled twice. What is the circumference of the wheel?

....

Maths skill 2: Calculating using the mathematics of shape

When working with shape the most common dimensions are:

- length: how long something is
- area: a measure of the size of a surface
- volume: a measure of three-dimensional space.

> **KEY WORDS**
>
> **area:** a measure of the size of a surface (measured in square units, for example cm² or m²)
>
> **volume:** a measure of three-dimensional space (measured in cubic units, for example cm³ or m³)

Area and volume values have units that require index notation. For example:

Area is always measured in square units: m² or cm².

$$m^2 = m \times m \qquad cm^2 = cm \times cm$$

Volume is always measured in cubic units: m³ or cm³.

$$m^3 = m \times m \times m \qquad cm^3 = cm \times cm \times cm$$

Table 6.3 shows some equations relating to shape that you will have met in maths.

Shape	Area of a rectangle	Area of a triangle	Area of a circle	Volume of a cuboid	Volume of a cylinder
Expression	length × width	$\frac{1}{2}$ base × height	πr^2, where r is the radius	length × width × height	$\pi r^2 h$, where h is the height
Units	m² or cm²	m² or cm²	m² or cm²	m³ or cm³	m³ or cm³

Table 6.3: Equations for the area and volume of some common shapes.

You can read more about volume in Chapter 1 of the Coursebook.

> **LOOK OUT**
>
> You need to be able to recall these equations and use them in calculations. Learn them.

WORKED EXAMPLE 6.2

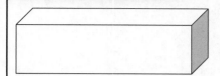

Figure 6.9: Rectangular container.

The rectangular container in Figure 6.9 is filled with water to a depth of 0.45 m. The container is 2.50 m long and 1.50 m across. Find the density of water in the container if the mass of the water is 1690 kg. Give your answer to 3 s.f.

Step 1: List the knowns and unknowns.

Knowns: length = 2.50 m, width = 1.50 m, height = 0.45 m, mass = 1690 kg

Unknowns: volume, density

Step 2: As the volume is part of the density equation, find the volume of hay first.

Volume of a cuboid is length × width × height.

Volume = 2.50 m × 1.50 m × 0.45 m = 1.69 m³

Step 3: Substitute mass and volume into the equation for density:

$$\rho = \frac{m}{v}$$

$$= \frac{1690\,\text{kg}}{1.69\,\text{m}^3} = 1000\,\text{kg/m}^3$$

Questions

3 Both of the shapes in Figure 6.10 has a mass of 240 g. Determine which of the shapes will exert the least pressure on the table. Circle A or B. Show your working.

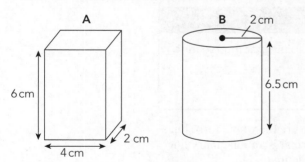

Figure 6.10: Two shapes with identical mass.

4   In a school playground a child is rotating a ball on a piece of string above her head at a height of 1.5 m (Figure 6.11). The radius of the rotation is 1.8 m. Other children need to keep clear to avoid accidents. How much space in cubic metres (m³) does the child need to give herself to spin the ball?

Take π = 3.14. Give your answer to 3 s.f.

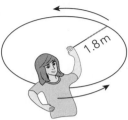

Figure 6.11: How much space is needed to spin the ball?

....

....

....

....

Maths focus 2: Drawing angles in ray diagrams

Angles of reflection and refraction are a measure of how much a light ray turns from its original path. It helps if you can visualise the way that the ray changes direction. Imagine you are facing along the original ray in the direction of travel. Then think about how much your body has to turn to be able to travel along the new line. In mathematics, this amount of turn is known as an **angle**.

KEY WORDS

angle: a measure of the amount of turn between two adjoining or intersecting lines; this may be determined, in degrees, using a protractor

perpendicular: at 90° to, or at right angles to

When measuring an angle turned by a light ray, we don't measure the whole turn, but the amount of turn from a line known as the *normal*. The normal is an imaginary line **perpendicular** (at 90°) to the surface where the ray strikes it (Figure 6.12).

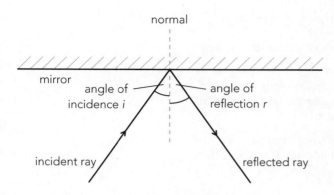

Figure 6.12: Angles of light rays relative to the normal.

What maths skills do you need to draw angles in ray diagrams?

1	Drawing and measuring angles	<ul><li>Identify the boundary between two surfaces where a change happens to a light ray</li><li>Know the convention for placing arrows on ray diagrams</li><li>Draw the normal, perpendicular to the surface where the ray hits it</li><li>Use a protractor to measure and to draw angles</li></ul>

Maths skills practice

How does drawing and measuring angles help in understanding the reflection and refraction of light?

Light travels in straight lines but when it meets a surface it often changes direction.

The change of direction happens because of *reflection* (the light bouncing off the surface) or *refraction* (the light changing speed and hence changing direction as it moves from one material into another).

Physicists need to be able to draw the rays of light so that they can work out where rays will travel and where images will be formed. For example, if a mirror is to be placed at a bend in the road so that drivers can see round the bend, it is important to know how the light rays will behave so that the mirror can be positioned correctly.

You can read more about the reflection and refraction of light in Chapter 13 of the Coursebook.

> **LOOK OUT**
>
> In a ray diagram, the direction of travel of the light is shown by an arrow on the ray.

Maths skill 1: Drawing and measuring angles

You need to be able to use a protractor correctly. For example, to measure an angle of reflection accurately on a ray diagram:

- Place your protractor so that 0° to 180° line on the protractor lies *along the normal*. The centre of the protractor must be exactly where the ray and the normal meet at the mirror (see Figure 6.13).

Angles in ray diagrams are measured from the normal line. You may need to draw the normal line. Use a protractor or a set-square to draw a dashed line at 90° to the surface where the light ray hits the surface, as shown in Figure 6.13.

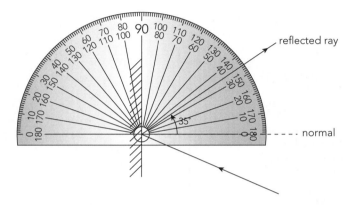

Figure 6.13: Measuring the angle of reflection using a protractor.

Read the angle of reflection on the protractor. It is the angle from the normal to the reflected ray.

WORKED EXAMPLE 6.3

Which diagram in Figure 6.14 correctly shows how light is reflected by a plane (flat) mirror?

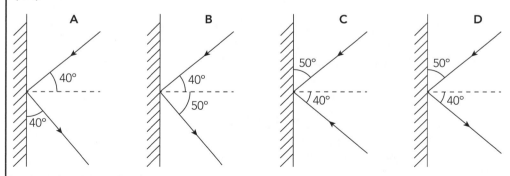

Figure 6.14: Which diagram shows how light is reflected by a plane mirror?

Step 1: Look for the incident and reflected rays. The incident ray arrow goes towards the mirror, then returns from the mirror as the reflected ray. This eliminates Diagram C.

CONTINUED

Step 2: Identify the normal. The normal is a line 90° to the surface where the ray strikes it.

Step 3: Work out any unknown angles on either side of the normal.

Step 4: Apply the rule of reflection:

angle of incidence = angle of reflection

Only D follows this rule, with the angle of incidence of 40°.

Practical Investigation 13.2 in the Practical Workbook involves measuring and recording angles of incidence to find the refractive index of glass.

Questions

5 A gardener wants to reflect light onto a statue in a shady part of her garden. She has decided to use a mirror to do this. The diagram shows an overhead view of the garden. A ray of light from the Sun at midday is shown.

Using a protractor, draw the normal line perpendicular to the surface of the mirror. Label it N. Then carefully draw and label the reflected ray.

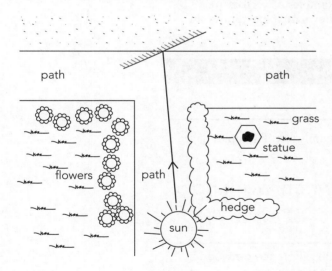

6 The diagram shows rays of light emerging from the flat surface of a pond. The angle of incidence is 32° and the angle of refraction is 45°. Use your protractor to find out which refracted ray has been drawn correctly. Circle A, B or C

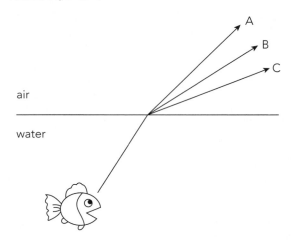

LOOK OUT

You will need to draw the normal line so that you can measure the angles.

Maths focus 3: Working with vectors

Vectors are variables that have direction as well as size. Examples of vectors are velocity, momentum, acceleration and force. A vector is shown on a diagram by an arrowed line showing its direction.

KEY WORD

scalar: a variable that has size (magnitude) only

Variables that are not vectors are called **scalars**. They have only size. Examples of scalars are mass, area, charge, speed and power.

What maths skills do you need when working with vectors?

1	Using vector diagrams	• Recognise the difference between a vector and a scalar
		• Draw vector diagrams to scale
		• Find the resultant of combining two vectors

Maths skill practice

How does working with vectors help to find the effect of several forces on an object?

If a side-wind prevents an aeroplane or a boat from going in the intended direction, it is important to know what the new direction will be. A vector diagram, representing the sizes and the directions of the forces involved, allows the combined effect to be found. The size of the *resultant vector*, and its angle to a reference direction, can be measured.

Maths skill 1: Using vector diagrams

KEY WORDS

scale diagram: a diagram in which all lengths are in the same ratio to the corresponding lengths in the actual object (to the same scale)

magnitude: the size of something

KEY WORD

resultant vector: the effective vector that results from combining two (or more) vectors. Resultants are shown by a double-headed arrow

You can read more about vectors in Chapter 3 of the Coursebook.

Question

7   State whether the physical quantities listed in the table are vectors or scalars

Physical quantity	Vector or scalar
Time taken for a ball to bounce	
Distance travelled by a car on a journey	
The change in velocity of a person on a zip wire	
The pressure inside a bicycle tube	
The acceleration of free fall	
The kinetic energy store of an aeroplane	

EXAM-STYLE QUESTIONS

1 a Underline all the vector quantities

    force   velocity   speed   weight

    distance   work   acceleration   **[2]**

  b Two students are pulling on a hoop. One student pulls east with a force of 30 N and the other student pulls north with a force of 40 N.

    Determine the resultant force on the hoop and its direction by drawing a scale diagram

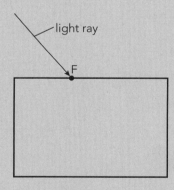

                                Force .... N   **[4]**

                                                   [Total: 6]

2 A ray of light is incident at point F on a rectangular glass block as shown in the diagram.

    light ray

    F

  a Using a ruler, draw a normal at point F.   **[1]**

  b Use a protractor to measure the angle of incidence (the angle between the normal and the incident ray).

    ....

    ....   **[1]**

  c Sketch the refracted ray with angle of refraction 15°.   **[1]**

                                                     [Total: 3]

CONTINUED

3   The diagram in Figure 6.21 shows a box with faces labelled P, Q and R.

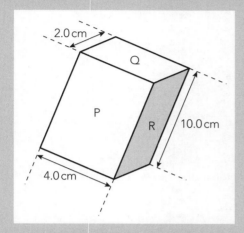

Figure 6.21: Box for question 3.

a   Which face of the box will be on the top when the box is placed on the floor to exert maximum pressure?

.... [1]

b   Calculate the surface area of the face P in m².

....

.... [2]

The mass of the box is 2.5 kg.

c   Calculate the pressure it exerts on the floor when face P is in contact with the floor. Give your answer in N/m² to 2 s.f.

....

....

....

4   An oil-filled container has a weight of 39.2 N. The mass of the empty container is 600 g. (Take $g = 9.8$ N/kg)

a   Determine the mass of the oil-filled container in grams.

....

.... [2]

b   State the mass of the oil in grams.

....

.... [1]

CONTINUED

The container has dimensions 20.0 cm × 10.0 cm × 20.0 cm.

c Calculate the volume of the container. Include the unit.

....

....

....

Volume of container = ... unit .... **[3]**

d Calculate the density of the oil. Give your answer to 2 s.f. Include the unit.

....

....

....

Density = ... unit .... **[3]**

[Total: 9]

5 The diagram shows a ray light that is shone from the bottom of a swimming pool. The angle x is less than the critical angle.

a On the diagram, sketch the refracted ray and label the angle of refraction, r. **[2]**

b Draw a diagram in the space below when angle x is greater than critical angle. Label the angle of reflection r.

[3]

[Total: 5]

› Applying more than one skill

Exam-style questions and sample answers have been written by the authors.

In examinations, the way in which marks are awarded may be different.

In all the questions, take $g = 9.8\,\text{N/kg}$.

1   A car sounds its horn. Which graph shows that the horn can be heard after 0.15 s when the car is 49 m away? Circle the correct answer

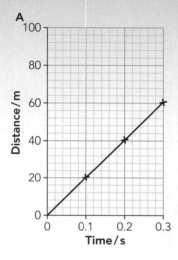

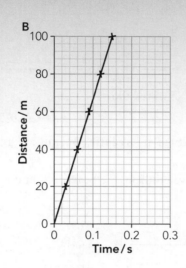

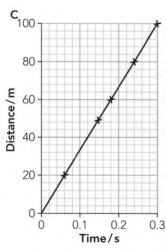

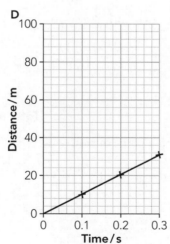

[Total marks: 1]

2 A stool has three legs. Each leg has a contact area with the ground of $2.5\,cm^2$.
The stool has a mass of $4\,kg$. A child of mass $41\,kg$ sits on the stool.

    a Calculate the pressure exerted on the floor

....

....

                  Pressure = ... unit .... **[4]**

    b The child tilts the stool slightly so that only two legs are in contact with
the ground.

       Determine the new pressure.

....

....

                  New pressure = ... **[3]**

                                               [Total marks: 7]

3 A $1\,m$ long beam has weight $120\,N$. It is pivoted at its centre. Weights are hung
from the beam as shown in the diagram.

Which is the correct option for hanging a weight from the beam so that it is
balanced. Circle A, B, C or D.

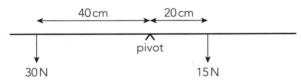

    A $20\,N$ at $45\,cm$ to the right of the pivot

    B $10\,N$ at $45\,cm$ to the right of the pivot

    C $45\,N$ at $15\,cm$ to the right of the pivot

    D $10\,N$ at $15\,cm$ to the left of the pivot

                                                   [Total marks: 1]

4 The diagram shows a ray of light reflected off a plane mirror.

    a Draw a normal to the mirror for this reflected ray. Label it **N**.   **[1]**

b Label and measure the angle of reflection. Find the angle of incidence. **[2]**

Angle of incidence =...........................

c Draw the incident ray **[1]**

[Total marks: 4]

5 A wagon of mass 1500 kg moving at 5.0 m/s collides with an identical wagon which is at rest. After collision they stick and move off together.

5.0 m/s

wagon 1   wagon 2 (at rest)

a Calculate the total momentum before the collision.

....

....

Total initial momentum = ... **[2]**

b Calculate the velocity of the wagons after the collision.

....

....

Velocity = ... m/s **[3]**

c Determine the kinetic energy transferred during the collision.

....

....

Kinetic energy transferred = ... kJ **[3]**

[Total marks: 8]

6 Two identical resistors each of $1.2\,k\Omega$ are connected to a 20 V battery as shown in the diagram.

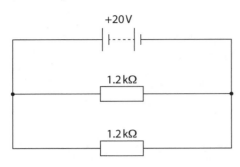

a Calculate the total resistance in the circuit.

....

....

Total resistance = ... **[3]**

b Calculate the current that flows through each resistor.

....

....

Current = ...mA **[3]**

c Calculate the amount of charge that flows through each resistor in 10 s.

....

....

Charge = ... Unit .... **[3]**

d The combination of two resistors is replaced by a lamp of 12 V, 60 W.

The lamp was turned on for 2 minutes. Calculate the energy transferred by the lamp.

....

....

....

Energy = ...kJ **[3]**

[Total marks: 12]

7 A 0.2 kW electric motor lifts 100 identical bricks each of mass 500 g.

a Calculate the work done by the motor in lifting the bricks to the height of 10 m.

....

....

Work done = ... **[3]**

b It takes 40 seconds to move the bricks up 10 m.

Calculate the energy transferred by the motor during this time.

....

....

Energy supplied = ... **[2]**

c In the space below, draw a Sankey diagram to show the energy transfer that takes place during this event. **[3]**

d Using your answer in part **c**, calculate the efficiency of the motor.

....

....

....

Efficiency = ... % **[2]**

[Total marks: 10]

8 A sample of radioactive material bismuth-214 undergoes radioactive decay by emitting an α-particle.

a The nuclear equation below shows the decay of bismuth.

Complete the equation by providing the missing numbers and letters **[3]**

$$^{214}_{.....}\text{Bi} \rightarrow \,^{.....}_{81}\text{Th} + \,^{4}_{2.....}$$

b The graph shows the decay of 100 g of bismuth-214.

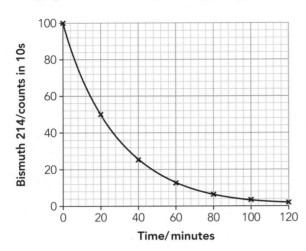

Determine the half-life of the nuclide in sample of the bismuth-214   **[2]**

....

....

c The count rate from background radiation was taken and found to be 10 counts per minute. Taking the background radiation into consideration, plot a corrected graph on the grid in **b**.   **[2]**

[Total marks: 7]

9 One light-year is the distance that light travels in one year.
The Andromeda galaxy is 2.537 million light-years away from the Earth.

a Calculate how long it takes for light to travel from Andromeda to Earth.   **[1]**

....

b Mars orbits the sun at an average distance of 2.28×10^8 km.
It takes 687 Earth days for Mars to orbit the Sun.
Calculate the average orbital speed of Mars.

....

....

....

Speed = ...   **[3]**

c   The speed of light is 3.0×10^8 m/s. Calculate how long it takes for light to reach Mars from the Sun. Give your answer in minutes.

....

....

....

Time = ... minutes   **[3]**

> Equations

Equations used only in the supplementary content of the extended syllabus are shown by the > to the left of the table.

General physics	
Word equation	**Symbol equation**
Speed = $\dfrac{\text{distance}}{\text{time}}$	$v = \dfrac{s}{t}$
Average speed = $\dfrac{\text{total distance}}{\text{total time}}$	
> Acceleration = $\dfrac{\text{change in velocity}}{\text{time taken}}$	$a = \dfrac{v - u}{t}$ $a = \dfrac{\Delta v}{\Delta t}$
Gravitational field strength = force per unit mass	$g = \dfrac{W}{m}$
Weight = mass × gravitational field strength	$W = mg$
Density = $\dfrac{\text{mass}}{\text{volume}}$	$\rho = \dfrac{m}{V}$
> Spring constant = force per unit extension	$k = \dfrac{F}{x}$
> Force = mass × acceleration	$F = ma$
Moment of a force = force × perpendicular distance	moment = Fd
> Momentum = mass × velocity	$p = mv$
> Impulse = change in momentum	$Ft = mv - mu$ $F\Delta t = \Delta(mv)$
> Resultant force = change in momentum over time	$F = \dfrac{\Delta p}{\Delta t}$
> Kinetic energy = $\dfrac{1}{2}$mass × velocity × velocity	$E_{\text{k}} = \dfrac{1}{2}mv^2$
> Change in gravitational potential energy = mass × gravitational field strength × change in height	$\Delta E_{\text{p}} = mg\Delta h$

Word equation	Symbol equation
Efficiency = $\dfrac{\text{useful power output}}{\text{total power input}} \times 100\%$	
Mechanical or electrical work done = energy transferred	$W = \Delta E$
Mechanical work done = force × distance moved	$W = Fd$
Power = $\dfrac{\text{change in energy}}{\text{time}}$	$P = \dfrac{\Delta E}{t}$
Power = $\dfrac{\text{work done}}{\text{time taken}}$	$P = \dfrac{W}{t}$
Pressure = $\dfrac{\text{force}}{\text{area}}$	$p = \dfrac{F}{A}$
Pressure = $\dfrac{\text{force}}{\text{area}}$	$p = \dfrac{F}{A}$
Change in pressure = density × gravitational field strength × change in depth	$\Delta p = \rho g \Delta h$

Thermal physics

Relationship between Celsius and Kelvin temperature scales	T (in K) = θ (in °C) + 273
Pressure × volume = constant	pV = constant
Specific heat capacity = energy required per unit mass per unit temperature increase	$c = \dfrac{\Delta E}{m\Delta\theta}$

Properties of waves, including light and sound

Velocity = frequency × wavelength	$v = f\lambda$
Angle of incidence = angle of reflection	$\angle i = \angle r$
Refractive index = ratio of sin $\angle i$ to sin $\angle r$	$n = \dfrac{\sin i}{\sin r}$
Refractive index = reciprocal sin critical angle	$n = \dfrac{1}{\sin c}$

Electricity and magnetism

Word equation	Symbol equation
In series: total resistance = sum of resistances	$R_T = R_1 + R_2$
In parallel: reciprocal of total resistance = sum of reciprocal resistances	$\frac{1}{R_T} = \frac{1}{R_1} + \frac{1}{R_2}$
Electromotive force (e.m.f.) = electrical work done by source per unit charge	$V = \frac{W}{Q}$
Potential difference (p.d.) = work done by a unit charge	$V = \frac{W}{Q}$
Current = $\frac{\text{charge}}{\text{time}}$	$I = \frac{Q}{t}$
Resistance = potential difference/current	$R = \frac{V}{I}$
Power = current × potential difference	$P = IV$
Energy = current × potential difference × time	$E = IVt$
Ratio of voltages across each resistor = ratio of their resistances	$\frac{R_1}{R_2} = \frac{V_1}{V_2}$
Ratio of primary to secondary potential differences = ratio of number of turns on the primary to the number of turns on the secondary	$\frac{V_p}{V_s} = \frac{N_p}{N_s}$
Current × potential difference across primary = current × potential difference across secondary	$I_p V_p = I_s V_s$
Power losses in cables = current squared × resistance	$P = I^2 R$

Space physics

Word equation	Symbol equation
Average orbital speed = $2 \times \pi \times \frac{\text{average radius of the orbit}}{\text{time period}}$	$V = \frac{2\pi r}{T}$
Hubble constant = $\frac{\text{speed at which galaxy moving away from Earth}}{\text{distance of galaxy from Earth}}$	$H_0 = \frac{v}{d}$

Word equation	Symbol equation
Distance of galaxy from Earth ÷ speed at which galaxy is moving away from Earth = reciprocal of Hubble constant = approximate age of the Universe	$\dfrac{d}{v} = \dfrac{1}{H_0}$
Area and volume	
Area of a rectangle	length × breadth
Area of a triangle	$\dfrac{1}{2}$base × height
Area of a circle	πr^2, where r is the radius
Volume of a cuboid	length × width × height
Volume of a cylinder	$\pi r^2 h$, where r is the radius and h is the height

> Glossary

Command Words

Below are the Cambridge International definitions for command words which may be used in exams. The information in this section is taken from the Cambridge Assessment International Education syllabus (0625/0972) for examination from 2023. You should always refer to the appropriate syllabus document for the year of your examination to confirm the details and for more information. The syllabus document is available on the Cambridge Assessment International Education website www.cambridgeinternational.org

calculate: work out from given facts, figures or information

comment: give an informed opinion

compare: identify/comment on similarities and/or differences

deduce: conclude from available information

define: give precise meaning

describe: state the points of a topic / give characteristics and main features

determine: establish an answer using the available information

explain: set out purposes or reasons / make the relationships between things evident / provide why and/or how and support with relevant evidence

give: produce an answer from a given source or recall/memory

identify: name / select / recognise

justify: support a case with evidence / argument

predict: suggest what may happen based on available information

sketch: make a simple freehand drawing showing the key features, taking care over proportions

state: express in clear terms

suggest: apply knowledge and understanding to situations where there are a range of valid responses in order to make proposals / put forward considerations

Key Words

accuracy: how close a value is to the true value

angle: a measure of the amount of turn between two adjoining or intersecting lines; this may be determined, in degrees, using a protractor

anomalous result: one of a series of repeated experimental results that is much larger or smaller than the others

area: a measure of the size of a surface (measured in square units, for example cm^2 or m^2)

axis: a reference line on a graph or chart, along which a scale represents values of a variable

bar charts: a chart with separated rectangular bars of equal width; the height (or length) of a bar represents the value of the variable

best-fit line: a straight line or a smooth curve drawn on a graph that passes through or close to as many as possible of the data points; it represents the best estimate of the relationship between the variables

BIDMAS: 'Brackets, Indices, Division/Multiplication, Addition/Subtraction', which is the order in which mathematical operations are done in a multi-step calculation

categorical data: data that can be grouped into categories (types) but not ordered

circumference: the distance around a circle

continuous data: data that can take any numerical value within a range

control variable: variable that is kept constant in an investigation

coordinates: values that determine the position of a data point on a graph, relative to the axes

decimal place: the place-value position of a number after a decimal point; the number 6.357 has three decimal places

dependent variable: the variable that is measured or observed in an investigation, when the independent variable is changed

diameter: a straight line connecting two points on a circle (or sphere) that passes through the centre

directly proportional: the relationship between two variables such that when one doubles, the other doubles; the graph of the two variables is a straight line through the origin

discrete data: data that can take only certain values

equation: a mathematical statement, using an '=' sign, showing that two expressions are equal; an equation that shows the relationship between variables

estimate: (find) an approximate value

extrapolate: extending the line of best fit on a graph beyond the range of the data, in order to estimate values not within the data set

gradient: the slope (steepness) of a line on a graph; it is calculated by dividing the vertical change by the horizontal change

independent variable: variable in an investigation that is changed by the experimenter

index: a small number that indicates the power; for example, the index 4 here shows that the 2 is raised to the power 4, which means four 2s multiplied together: $2^4 = 2 \times 2 \times 2 \times 2$

intercept: the point at which a line on a graph crosses one of the axes; usually refers to the intercept with the vertical (y-) axis

interpolate: on a graph, to estimate the value of a variable from the value of the other variable, using a best-fit line. On a scale, to estimate a measurement that falls between two scale marks

intersect: where two lines on a graph meet or cross one another

inversely proportional: the relationship between two variables such that when one doubles, the other halves

line graph: a graph of one variable against another where the data points fall on or close to a single line, which may be straight, curved, or straight-line segments between points, depending on the relationship between the variables

linear relationship: a relationship between two variables that can be represented on a graph by a straight line

magnitude: the size of something

mean: an average value: the sum of a set of values divided by the number of values in the set

meniscus: the curved surface of a liquid in a tube or cylinder

negative relationship: when one variable decreases as the other increases

order of magnitude: the approximate size of a number, often given as a power of 10; for example, the order of magnitude of 2700 is 10^3

origin: the point on a graph at which the value of both variables is zero and where the axes cross

outlier: a value in a data set, or point on a graph, that is considered unusual compared with the trend of other values

parallelogram: a four-sided figure with two pairs of equal opposite sides, which are parallel

percentage: a fraction expressed out of 100, e.g. $\frac{1}{2} = \frac{50}{100} = 50\%$

perpendicular: at 90° to, or at right angles to

pie charts: a circular chart that is divided into sectors which represent the relative values of components; the angle of the sector is proportional to the value of the component x

positive relationship: when one variable increases as the other increases

power: a number raised to the power 2 is squared (e.g. x^2); a number raised to the power 3 is cubed (e.g. x^3); and so on

power of ten: a number such as 10^3 or 10^{-3}

precision: the closeness of agreement between several measured values obtained by repeated measurements; the precision of a single value can be indicated by the number of significant figures given in the number, for example 4.027 has greater precision (is more precise) than 4.0

processed data: data produced by calculation using raw experimental data

product: the result of multiplying two or more values

qualitative data: data that are descriptive and not numerical

quantitative data: data that are numerical

radius: the distance from the centre of a circle (or sphere) to the circle (or sphere surface)

random errors: measurement error that varies in an unpredictable way from one measurement to the next

range: the interval between a lowest value and a highest value, for example of a measured variable or on the scale of a measuring instrument

rate: a measure of how much one variable changes relative to another variable; usually how quickly a variable changes as time progresses

ratio: a comparison of two numbers or two measurements with the same unit. The ratio A to B can be written $A:B$ or expressed as a fraction $\frac{A}{B}$

raw data: data collected by measurement or observation

rearrange: to manipulate an equation mathematically so that the unknown value can be calculated; also termed 'change the subject'

precision: the smallest change in a value that can be observed on a measuring instrument

resultant vector: the effective vector that results from combining two (or more) vectors. Resultants are shown by a double-headed arrow

rounding: expressing a number as an approximation, with fewer significant figures; for example, 7.436 rounded to two significant figures is 7.4, or rounded to three significant figures it is 7.44

Sankey diagram: a diagram that shows all the energy transfers taking place in an energy conversion process; the thickness of the arrow determines the amount of energy involved

scale: a set of marks with equal intervals, for example on a graph axis or a measuring cylinder; or, on a scale diagram, the ratio of a length in the diagram to the actual size

scale diagram: a diagram in which all lengths are in the same ratio to the corresponding lengths in the actual object (to the same scale)

scalar: a variable that has size (magnitude) only

scientific notation: another term for standard form

significant figures: the number of digits in a measurement, not including any zeros at the beginning; for example, the number of significant figures in 0.0682 is three

standard form: notation in which a number is written as a number between 1 and 10 multiplied by a power of 10; for example, 4.78×10^9; also called scientific notation, or standard index form, or standard notation

surface area: the total area of the surface of a three-dimensional object

systematic error: measurement error that results in measured values differing from the true value by the same amount each time a measurement is made; this may occur for example when a balance reads 0.02 g with no mass on it

trend: a pattern shown by data; on a graph this may be shown by points following a 'trend line', the best estimate of this being the best-fit line

uncertainty: range of variation in experimental results because of sources of error; the true value is expected to be within this range

unit: a standard used in measuring a variable, for example the metre or the volt

unit prefix: a prefix (term added to the front of a word) added to a unit name to indicate a power of 10 of that unit, e.g. 1 millimetre = 10^{-3} metre

variable: the word used for any measurable quantity; its value can vary or change

vector: a variable that has a magnitude (size) and a direction

volume: a measure of three-dimensional space (measured in cubic units, for example cm^3 or m^3)

Acknowledgements

The authors and publishers acknowledge the following sources of copyright material and are grateful for the permissions granted.

Thanks to the following for permission to reproduce images:

Cover scotspencer/Getty Images;

slowmotiongli/Getty Images; MaxOzerov/Getty Images; dimid_86/Getty Images